Jesus Christ in the Eucharistic:
A Series of Eucharistic Miracles

Rayfiel G Mychal

Copyright © 2019

All rights reserved.

DEDICATION:

THIS BOOK IS DEDICATED TO MSGR. FR. JIM C. GEHL, MY MOM (WHO IS ALSO NAMED MARY), EVERYBODY OUT THERE WITH THE NAME MARY AND TO THE VIRGIN MARY.

Table of Contents

Table of Contents iv

Before the Stories 2

The Establishment of the Eucharist 5

The Miracle of Siena, Italy 7

The Miracle of Amsterdam 8

The Miracle of Blanot, France 9

The Miracle at Bolsena-Orvieto, Italy 11

The Miracle of Lanciano 12

The Miracle of Chirattakonam, India 13

The Miracle of Santarem 14

The Miracle of Sokolka 16

The Miracle in Legnica 17

The Miracle of Tixtla, Mexico 18

The Miracle in Buenos Aires, Argentina 19

The Miracle in Betania, Venezuela 20

The Miracle of Montserrat, Spain 21

The Miracle of the Island of Tumaco, Colombia 22

The Miracle of Weiten-Raxendorf, Austria 23

The Miracle of Bordeaux, France 24

The Miracle of Eten, Peru 25

The Miracle at Bruges, Belgium 26

The Miracle of Cascia, Italy 27

Eucharistic Miracle at Herkenrode-Hasselt 28

The Eucharistic Miracle of Augsburg, Germany 30

The Eucharistic Miracle of Middleburg-Louvain 32

The Miracle at Bois-Seigneur-Isaac 33

The Miracle of Brussels, Belgium 35

The Miracle of Fiecht 36

The Miracle of Ludbreg 37

The Miracle of Herentals 39

The Miracle of Morne-Rouge 41

The Miracle of Scete 42

The Miracle of Herentals 44

The Miracle of Avignon 46

The Miracle of Dijon 48

The Miracle of Douai 50

The Miracle of Faverney 52

The Miracle of La Rochelle 55

The Miracle of Les Ulmes 57

The Miracle of Marseille-En-Beauvais 59

The Miracle of Paris 61

The Miracle of Pressac 63

The Miracle of Ettiswil 65

The Miracle of Saint-André 67

The Miracles of Benningen 69

The Miracle of Bettbrunn 71

The Miracle of Erding 73

The Miracle of Kranenburg 76

The Miracle of Regensburg 78

The Miracle of Walldürn 80

The Miracle of Wilsnack 82

The Miracles of Altari 84

The Miracles of Asti of 1535 86

The Miracles of Asti of 1718 86

The Miracle of Bagno di Romagna 88

The Miracle of Cava dei Tirreni 89

The Miracle of Dronero 90

The Miracle of Ferrara 91

The Miracles of Florence 92

The Miracle of Turin 94

The Miracle of Gruaro 95

The Miracle of Macerata 97

The Miracle of Rimini 98

The Miracle of Mogoro 100

The Miracle of Offida 102

The Miracles of Rome 104

The Miracle with St. Peter Damian 106

The Miracles of Scala 107

The Miracles of Salzano 108

The Miracles of Trani 109

The Miracles of Veroli 110

The Miracles of Volterra 111

The Miracle of Alkmaar 112

The Miracle of Boxmeer 113

The Miracle of Bergen 114

The Miracles of Meerssen 115

The Miracle of Stiphout 116

The Miracle of Glotowo 117

The Miracle of Krakow 118

The Miracle of Poznan 119

The Miracle of Assisi 121

The Miracle of Alboraya-Almácera 122

The Miracle of Alcoy 124

The Miracle of Caravaca de la Cruz 126

The Miracle of Cimballa 128

The Miracle of Daroca 129

The Miracle of Gerona 131

The Miracle of Gorkum - El Escorial 133

The Miracle of Guadalupe 134

The Miracle of Ivorra 136

The Miracle of Moncada 137

The Miracle of O'Cebreiro 140

The Miracle of Silla 142

The Miracle of Zaragoza 143

The Bread of Life 145

Before the Stories

The foundation for Catholics to be united with Jesus is through the Holy Eucharist. As Catholics, we are asked to believe that the Eucharist is what unites us to Jesus. This is because Jesus remains on earth in body, blood, soul, and divinity.

Many people, both Catholics, and many other people find it hard to believe that a flat piece of bread and wine are actually the Body and Blood of Christ. It is hard to grasp that bread and wine are turned into Jesus since there isn't anything miraculous that we can see.

There aren't any light shows or angelic hymns as the bread and wine are transformed into the Body and Blood of Jesus. However, it is very important that we venerate and worship Jesus in the Eucharist even though we can't see Jesus' body, blood, soul, and divinity.

Let us go back to the beginning, on the Last Supper, Jesus instituted the sacrament of the Eucharist to celebrate His death and resurrection. Jesus was going to die and ascend into Heaven so He wanted to remain with us until the end of time. Jesus preached the miracle of the Eucharist to His followers when He said, "'I am the living bread that came down from heaven; whoever eats this bread will live forever; and the bread that I will give is my flesh for the life of the world. For my flesh is true food, and my blood is true drink'" (John 6:51-55).

Just like today, people didn't understand what Jesus meant and many of them turned away because they found it difficult to grasp. However, the sacrament of the Mass and the celebration of the Eucharist is a remembrance and Jesus' eternal offering and sacrifice.

To join Jesus more intimately, He left Himself as food and drink to unite Himself to us spiritually and physically. This unites us, not only to Jesus but also unites us with God the Father and the Holy Spirit.

Therefore, every time that we receive the Holy Eucharist, we grow closer to the Holy Trinity. Not only that but consuming Christ's flesh avails much, it is the reason why Jesus became flesh and died for us. Not only that, but the Eucharist/ Body and Blood strengthened Jesus during His passion since He knew that His body would save humanity.

Concepcion Cabrera de Armida had visions of Jesus where He felt extreme consolation and relief that Jesus felt when He left Himself in the Holy Eucharist.

During His passion, Jesus found consolation at the thought of giving us strength through the Holy Eucharist. Jesus' pain and fear were diminished by the devotion that we have to the Holy Eucharist. When Jesus was being scourged, He rejoiced that His body was being grounded like wheat and His blood was being pressed like grapes in the winepress.

Therefore, as remaining behind as bread and wine, He was able to extend His lifespan here on earth. Furthermore, the Eucharist represents the new covenant of everlasting life between God and humanity that makes us one with Jesus. [1]

---

[1] "The Eucharist Sacrifice and Sacrament." The Real Presence Eucharistic. <http://www.therealpresence.org/eucharst/intro/a11.html>. January 16, 2019.

"Christ in the Eucharist." Catholic Answers. <https://www.catholic.com/tract/christ-in-the-eucharist>. January 16, 2019.

"Questions on the Most Blessed Sacrament 1." Real Presence Eucharistic Education and Adoration Association. <http://www.therealpresence.org/eucharst/tes/a7.html>. January 16, 2019.

Fay. Monsignor William P. "The Real Presence of Jesus Christ in the Sacrament in the Sacrament of the Eucharist: Basic Questions and Answers." *Order of the Mass.* United Conference of Catholic Bishops. <http://www.usccb.org/prayer-and-worship/the-mass/order-of-mass/liturgy-of-the-eucharist/the-real-presence-of-jesus-christ-in-the-sacrament-of-the-eucharist-basic-questions-and-answers.cfm>. January 16, 2019.

Foley, Stephanie. "The Real Presence of Jesus in the Eucharist." Relevant Radio. July 15, 2018. <https://relevantradio.com/2018/07/real-presence-jesus-eucharist/>. January 16, 2019.

The Establishment of the Eucharist

The Eucharist was first established during the Last Supper before Jesus was crucified on the Cross. It happened when it was almost Passover and as the tradition for the Jewish people, Jesus and His Apostles also went to Jerusalem.

They went up to a room of a friend who also followed Jesus. Jesus and His Apostles spent time in the room socializing and celebrating the special holiday of Passover.

However, Jesus knew that this was going to be the last time that they all gathered together and celebrated. He knew that that very night, He was going to be betrayed, arrested, and crucified the following day.

He decided that it was time for Him to institute the Bread of the Angels.

"When the hour had come, He sat down, and the twelve apostles with Him. Then He said to them, 'With *fervent* desire I have desired to eat this Passover with you before I suffer; for I say to you, I will no longer eat of it until it is fulfilled in the kingdom of God.'

Then He took the cup, and gave thanks, and said, 'Take this and divide *it* among yourselves; for I say to you, I will not drink of the fruit of the vine until the kingdom of God comes.'

And He took bread, gave thanks and broke *it,* and gave *it* to them, saying, 'This is My body which is given for you; do this in remembrance of Me.'

Likewise He also *took* the cup after supper, saying, 'This cup *is* the new covenant in My blood, which is shed for you.'"

(Luke 22:14-19)

The Apostles didn't know what this meant at that time but they paid close attention to Jesus' words.

Jesus was going to die, but He wanted to stay behind for generations so He instituted the Eucharist: The Bread of the Angels.

From that day forward, the angels would remain praising and adoring God in the Holy Eucharist for all time. At the same time, Jesus would remain with us in body and blood after His death and resurrection. [2]

---

[2] King James Bible Online

Mychal, Rayfiel G. *Angels Throughout the Bible: The Story of the Unsung Heroes.* September 2017.

The Miracle of Siena, Italy

On August 14, 1730, thieves broke into the Church of St. Francis and stole the ciborium that contained hundreds of Hosts. The crime happened as the people were celebrating the eve of the Assumption. The theft was discovered the following morning and there was an immediate search for the Hosts.

The bishop asked for prayers and reparations to God for forgiveness. Two days later, a parishioner in a neighboring church found a bright light coming from the collection box. When the collection box was opened, the priests found the Hosts but they were covered by dirt ad cobwebs. The priests usually consumed the Hosts that were desecrated but since they were dirty, they decided to let them decompose naturally. The Hosts should've decomposed in a few weeks, however, it was discovered that the Hosts were intact. Up to today, the Hosts remain fresh with a sweet-smelling aroma. The Hosts are preserved in Siena in the Basilica of St. Francis where they are displayed publicly. [3]

---

[3] Callum. "5 Incredible Eucharistic Miracles from the last 25 years." Diocese of Westminster. January 6, 2016. (http://dowym.com/voices/5-incredible-eucharistic-miracles-from-the-last-25-years/). January 17, 2019.

"Siena, Italy: Saint Catherine of Siena and the Eucharistic Miracle of Siena." *Eucharistic Miracles: Tangible Signs of the Real Presence of Christ in the Eucharist.* The Catholic Travel Guide. (https://thecatholictravelguide.com/destinations/italy/siena-italy-saint-catherine-siena-eucharistic-miracle-siena/). January 17, 2019.

The Miracle of Amsterdam

The miracle of Amsterdam happened on March 15, 1345. On that day, there was a man who was on his sick bed. The parish priest arrived to give him the Last Rites and Holy Communion. However, the man was sick so he vomited the Host. His caretaker swept it up and threw it into the fireplace.

The next morning, the caretaker noticed that the Host was floating above the flames. The woman was afraid but she approached the Host and placed it on a clean linen cloth and placed into a linen chest. The woman called the priest in St. Nicholas Church, to give him the host. The following day, the priest found the Host again in the linen chest at the sick man's house. The priest found it odd but he didn't think twice about it so he took the Host back to St. Nicholas church.

On the third day, the priest discovered that the Host was in the linen chest again. The priest realized that it was a Eucharistic Miracle that God wanted him to share. The priest consulted his superiors and they decided to take the Host back to the sick man's house to hold a procession towards the church. [4]

---

[4] "The Eucharistic Miracle of Amsterdam." *Eucharistic Miracles: Tangible Signs of the Real Presence of Christ in the Eucharist*. The Catholic Travel Guide.
(https://thecatholictravelguide.com/destinations/netherlands-holland/eucharistic-miracle-amsterdam/). January 17, 2019.

The Miracle of Blanot, France

The miracle that took place happened on Easter Sunday in 1331.

During Communion, two altar servers approached the altar railing, took their place at the end, and turned the cloth over the railing. The people took their places and held out their hands under the cloth as they received Holy Communion.

The last person to receive Communion was a woman named Jacquette. The priest placed the Host on her tongue and began to walk back to the altar. The two altar servers and those around her saw that the woman had accidentally drop the Host into the cloth that covered her hands.

As the priest was placing the ciborium inside the Tabernacle, one of the altar servers approached him to tell him about the accident. The priest immediately returned to the railing to retrieve the Host. However, instead of finding the Host, he saw that the Host had dissolved into a spot of blood.

After Mass, the priest took the cloth into the sacristy and placed the stained area into a basin filled with water. However, the more he washed the cloth, the bigger and darker the stain became.

Not only that but he saw that the water had also turned bloody.

The priest and his assistants were frightened and cried out, "'This is the Precious Blood of our Lord Jesus Christ.'" (Choosing Him. No pag.)

The priest took a knife and cut the piece of the cloth that was imprinted by the Host. The priest placed the cloth in the tabernacle and kept the Hosts that were distributed on that Sunday aside so that they would be preserved.

The Hosts have been preserved more than 375 years and are taken in a procession around the church of Blanot every year on the anniversary of the miracle. [5]

---

[5] "Eucharistic Miracle: Blanot, France – 1331." Choosing Him. July 12, 2015. (http://choosing-him.blogspot.com/2015/07/eucharistic-miracle-blanot-france-1331.html). January 17, 2019.

The Miracle at Bolsena-Orvieto, Italy

In 1263, a German priest, Pater of Prague was on a pilgrimage to Rome. Even though Father Peter was very pious and religious, he had trouble believing that Jesus was actually present in the Eucharist.

While on his way to Rome, he celebrated Mass at the tomb of St. Christina. As he began to speak the words of Consecration, blood began to pour out from the Host and into his hands.

The priest was confused so he immediately ran to Pope Ur to report the incident. The pope ordered the Bishop of the diocese to bring the Host and linen cloth that had the blood to Orvieto. The Church officials held a procession where they carried the relics to the Cathedral of Orvieto where they were exhibited. [6]

---

[6] "Bolsena-Orvieto, Italy." *Eucharistic Miracles*. The Real Presence: Christ in the Eucharist. (http://www.therealpresence.org/eucharst/mir/bolsena.html). January 17, 2019.

The Miracle of Lanciano

In the 8th century, there was a priest in the Church of Legontian in Lanciano, Italy.

The priest had a hard time believing that Jesus was actually present in the Eucharist. As he was reciting the consecration, he saw that the bread and wine were transformed into real human flesh and blood. The blood coagulated into five globules.

News of the miracle spread and an investigation quickly took place that approved the miracle.

In 1971, an investigation concluded that the flesh was cardiac tissue and the blood was fresh instead of being 1200 years old (when the miracle took place). The precious body and blood of Christ was displaced in the Church of San Francesco in Lanciano, Italy. [7]

---

[7] Pop Church Editor. "5 Extraordinary Eucharistic Miracles that Left Physical Evidence (With Pictures!)." June 28, 2015. (https://churchpop.com/2015/06/28/5-extraordinary-eucharistic-miracles-with-pictures/). January 17, 2019.

The Miracle of Chirattakonam, India

On April 28, 2001, the parish church of Saint Mary in Chirattakonam witnessed a Eucharistic Miracle. The story began when the church began a Novena to St. Jude Thaddeus. At 8:49 am, the priest exposed the Blessed Sacrament for adoration.

After a few moments, the priest began to see three dots on the Host. The priest stopped praying and began to look at the monstrance and invited the congregation to approach the altar so that they could witness the three dots. The priest asked the congregation to remain in adoration while he went to the archbishop to inform him of the event.

When the priest returned, he opened the tabernacle and saw that the three dots were clearer and formed the face of Jesus crowned with thorns. The miracle was investigated **His Beatitude Cyril Mar Baselice, archbishop of the diocese of Trivandrum. Once the event was confirmed as a miracle, the Host was placed in the monstrance and placed in the** Saint Mary in Chirattakonam.[8]

"4 Amazing Eucharistic Miracles From the Last 20 years." Aletia. (https://aletcia.org/2018/02/27/4-amazing-eucharistic-miracles-from-the-last-20-years/5/). January 18, 2019.

"The Miracle of Chirattakonam, India – 21st century." *5 Extraordinary Eucharistic Miracles that Left Physical Evidence (With Pictures!)*. Church Pop Editor. June 28, 2015.
(https://churchpop.com/2015/06/28/5-extraordinary-eucharistic-miracles-with-pictures/). January 18, 2019.

The Miracle of Santarem

In the 13th century, a woman in Santarém, Portugal, was in distress because she thought that her husband was cheating on her. To find out if her suspicions were correct, she went to a sorceress for advice. The sorceress told her that the price for the consultation was a consecrated Host.

The following day, she went to the Church of Stephen to attend church. When the woman received Holy Communion, the woman stole the Host and hid it in her veil. As soon as she took the Host, it began to bleed. It bled so much that the other people thought that she had cut her hand. When she returned home, she threw the bloody Host in an old trunk on her bedroom.

That night, a mysterious light shone through the trunk. The couple woke up and that is when the wife told her husband what she had done.

As soon as they realized that the light was coming out from the Host, they both knelt to adore and repent for the sacrilegious act.

The following morning, the couple went to the local priest and told him what had happened. The priest followed them to their home and placed the Host in a wax container. The priest and the couple solemnly returned to the Church of St. Stephen.

When the priest opened the tabernacle, he found out that the wax container was shattered into many pieces.

So the priest immediately placed the Host in an enclosed crystal pix.

After the miracle was approved, the Church of St. Stephen was renamed to the Church of the Holy Miracle and the Host was placed there for display. [9]

"The Eucharistic Miracle of Santarém – 13th century." *5 Extraordinary Eucharistic Miracles that Left Physical Evidence (With Pictures!)*. Church Pop Editor. June 28, 2015. (https://churchpop.com/2015/06/28/5-extraordinary-eucharistic-miracles-with-pictures/). January 18, 2019.

"Santarem, Portugal: Eucharistic Miracle of Santarem." The Catholic Travel Guide. (https://thecatholictravelguide.com/destinations/portugal-catholic-shrines-places-interest/santarem-eucharistic-miracle/). January 18, 2019.

The Miracle of Sokolka

On October 12, 2008, a parish priest, Fr. Stanislaw Gniedziejko, accidentally dropped a Host during the distribution of Holy Communion.

The priest paused distributing communion, picked up the Host, and placed it on a container of water. At the end of Mass, the priest asked the sacristan, Sr. Julia, to place the Host into a bigger container.

A week later, Sr. Julia noticed the sweet aroma of unleavened bread. She opened the container and found the Host, which was still intact with a bright red stain.

The Host was bleeding but it did not tainted the water. The Host was taken to two different scientists and they concluded that the structure of the Host was identical to the myocardial tissue (heart tissue) of a living person. The structure of the heart muscle fibers were intertwined with the bread. [10]

---

[10] "5 Incredible Eucharistic Miracles from the last 25 Years." Diocese of Westminster. January 6, 2016. (http://dowym.com/voices/5-incredible-eucharistic-miracles-from-the-last-25-years/). January 18, 2019.

"4 Amazing Eucharistic miracles from the last 20 years." Aleteia. January 19. (https://aleteia.org/2018/02/27/4-amazing-eucharistic-miracles-from-the-last-20-years/3/). January 18, 2019.

The Miracle in Legnica

On December 25, 2013, while distributing Holy Communion, a Host fell on the floor.

The Host was immediately picked up and placed in a container with water to dissolve. However, instead of dissolving, it turned red.

An investigation began and a tiny red fragment was taken from the Host. The result of the investigation determined that the Host had fragments of tissue that were found contained the fragmented part of the cross striated muscle. That muscle is similar to the heart muscle but with alterations that appear during the agony.

The Congregation of the Doctrine of the Faith, from the Vatican, advised that the Host should be exposed to the public.

Today, the Host is publicly on display in the St. Jack Parish in Legnica. [11]

---

[11] "4 Amazing Eucharistic miracles from the last 20 years." (https://aletcia.org/2018/02/27/4-amazing-eucharistic-miracles-from-the-last-20-years/2/). January 19, 2019.

" Legnica, Poland: Eucharistic Miracle in St. Jack Church (St. Hyacinth)." The Catholic Travel Guide. (https://thecatholictravelguide.com/destinations/poland/legnica-poland-eucharistic-miracle-st-jack-church-st-hyacinth/). January 19, 2019.

The Miracle of Tixtla, Mexico

During a parish retreat on October 21, 2006 a retreat was taking place in Tixtla, Mexico. While at the retreat, the priest was distributing Holy Communion.

Suddenly, he noticed that one of the Hosts had a reddish substance. He placed the Host aside and the bishop, Most Reverend Alejo Zavala Castor, commissioned investigation an investigation.

The investigation concluded that the red stain was blood with DNA that Hemoglobin of human origin. The blood came from inside the Host and the blood type was AB (the same type that is found in other Eucharistic miracles and in the Holy Shroud of Turin).

Further investigations showed that the blood outside the Host had coagulated but the underlying internal layers contained the presence of fresh blood (which meant that the Host was still bleeding). [12]

---

[12] "5 Incredible Eucharistic Miracles from the last 25 Years." Callum. Diocese of Westminster. January 6, 2016. (http://dowym.com/voices/5-incredible-eucharistic-miracles-from-the-last-25-years/). January 19, 2019.

"4 Amazing Eucharistic miracles from the last 20 years." Aleteia. (https://aleteia.org/2018/02/27/4-amazing-eucharistic-miracles-from-the-last-20-years/4/). January 19, 2019.

The Miracle in Buenos Aires, Argentina

The miracle in Buenos Aires showed the sufferings of Jesus while He was crucified.

When the priest was consecrating the Host, he noticed that it began to bleed. The Host had become part of human tissue that was part of a heart, a muscle of the myocardium, which is the left ventricle, the muscle that gives life to the whole heart and body.

However, the tissue revealed that it belonged to a person who had gone through intense pain. The pain that It was in, reflected extensive periods of time where a person could hardly breath. The pain was an immense strain that put on the heart and had been stabbed on the left side. Both of these pains and wounds reflected the suffering that Jesus experienced during the crucifixion. Therefore, this kind of pain was so intense that it should've killed the person who was experienced it.

However, the tissue showed signs of still alive. This proved that the intact white blood cells were still alive and that the heart was pulsating. [13]

---

[13] "5 Incredible Eucharistic Miracles from the last 25 Years." Callum. Diocese of Westminster. (http://dowym.com/voices/5-incredible-eucharistic-miracles-from-the-last-25-years/). January 19, 2019.

The Miracle in Betania, Venezuela

The Eucharistic miracle of Venezuela took place at the Marian Shrine of Finca Betania in 1991. During Mass, the priest had divided the big Host into four parts and consumed one of them. However, when he looked down at the paten (a plate where the Hosts are kept) ho noticed that one of the pieces had a red spot. From that spot, blood was coming out as if it was a fresh wound. Those who present at the church saw the miracle and confirmed that the blood didn't come out of the priest.

The studies of the blood showed that the blood did not match the blood type of the priest. Not only that, but the blood type was AB positive and from a living heart, just like all the other miracles and the Shroud of Turin. The Host continually produce fresh blood from within ever since. The Host was placed in the convent of the Augustianian Recollects Nuns of the Sacred Heart of Jesus in Los Teques for public viewing. In 1998, a man went on a pilgrimage to see the Host for himself. After Mass, he saw that the Host was a pulsating heart that was bleeding from inside. The man reported that the Host looked as if it was in flames. [14]

---

[14] "5 Incredible Eucharistic Miracles from the last 25 Years." Callum. Diocese of Westminster. (http://dowym.com/voices/5-incredible-eucharistic-miracles-from-the-last-25-years/). January 19, 2019.

Galeone, Christine. "7 Amazing Eucharistic Miracles." Beliefnet. (https://www.beliefnet.com/faiths/catholic/7-amazing-eucharistic-miracles.aspx?p=7). January 19, 2019.

The Miracle of Montserrat, Spain

A different kind of Eucharistic miracle happened in 1657 at the Monastery of Our Lady of Montserrat.

A young girl begged the Abbot of the monastery, Don Millán de Mirando, to celebrate three Masses for her father. The girl believed that saying three Masses would free her father from Purgatory.

The Abbot was moved by the girl's pain so he celebrated the Masses for him.

During the consecration of the Eucharist of the first Mass, the girl saw her father kneeling among the flames at the step of the altar. Those around her asked her to put a tissue near the flames that she could only see.

However, the tissue began to burn.

During the second Mass, the girl saw her dad dressed in a colorful suit and standing next to the deacon.

After the third Mass, the girl saw her dad wearing a white suit and rising into the sky. The girl thanked the monks for helping her dad go to Heaven. [15]

---

[15] Galeone, Christine. "7 Amazing Eucharistic Miracles." Beliefnet. (https://www.beliefnet.com/faiths/catholic/7-amazing-eucharistic-miracles.aspx?p=2). January 19, 2019.

The Miracle of the Island of Tumaco, Colombia

In 1906, an earthquake caused tsunamis that destroyed many cities and killed at least 500 people along the coasts of Colombia.

When the water began to rise and reached the inland, the people ran to the church and asked him to lead a procession with the Eucharist.

With extreme faith and courage, the priest consumed all of the Hosts, except for one. Then he placed the last one in the monstrance. The priest led the procession and they all asked God to have pity on them. The procession went all the way to the shore and people began to weep and cry out to God to have mercy on them.

Waves continued to rush towards them but the priest raised the Blessed Sacrament and traced the sign of the cross.

Immediately, the tsunami stopped and the waters receded. The people thanked God in the Blessed Sacrament for His mercy and for saving their lives.[16]

---

[16] Galeone, Christine. "7 Amazing Eucharistic Miracles." Beliefnet. (https://www.beliefnet.com/faiths/catholic/7-amazing-eucharistic-miracles.aspx?p=3). January 19, 2019.

The Miracle of Weiten-Raxendorf, Austria

In 1411, a thief stole a consecrated Host from the church in Weiten.

The thief hid the Host in his glove and took off on his horse.

However, after some time, the horse stopped and wouldn't ride any farther. The man did everything to get the horse to move, even beating it.

Bystanders didn't know the man's intentions but jumped in to help the thief get back on his horse. The horse shook so much that it caused the Host to fall out of the man's glove without him noticing.

A few days later, a woman found the Host on the ground. However, the Host was encircled in a bright light and was broken in two but joined together by bleeding threads of flesh. She informed the priest and the news of the event spread.

Soon, a large church was built to thank God. [17]

---

[17] Galeone, Christine. "7 Amazing Eucharistic Miracles." Beliefnet. (https://www.beliefnet.com/faiths/catholic/7-amazing-eucharistic-miracles.aspx?p=43). January 19, 2019.

The Miracle of Bordeaux, France

In 1822, a different kind of Eucharistic miracle happened in the Church of St. Eulalia in Rue Mazarin, Bordeaux. The miracle happened almost two years after the Holy Family of Bordeaux opened.

As soon as the Abbot gave the benediction with the Blessed Sacrament, Jesus appeared to him and all those present inside the Host. The priest reported that when he saw Jesus, he could see His whole body (head, chest, arms) in the middle of a glowing circle.

Jesus looked like He was in His thirties. He was dressed in a white tunic with a dark red scarf draped over His shoulder.

Jesus stood in front of everybody for more than twenty minutes. Jesus smiled at everybody and began to raise His right hand to bless them with His right hand.

Some people reported that they heard Jesus say, "'I Am He Who Is.'" (Galeone, no pag.)

Since then, people have been visiting the chapel to venerate the monstrance where Jesus appeared. [18]

---

[18] Galeone, Christine. "7 Amazing Eucharistic Miracles." Beliefnet. (https://www.beliefnet.com/faiths/catholic/7-amazing-eucharistic-miracles.aspx?p=5). January 19, 2019.

The Miracle of Eten, Peru

In 1649, Jesus appeared twice to crowds of people and to Jerome de Silva Manrique.

During exposition on the Feast of Corpus Christi, Jesus appeared to those present in the Blessed Sacrament in the form of a child.

On the second apparition, Jesus appeared in the Host to those present during the exposition of the Blessed Sacrament as a child.

The supervisor of the convent where the miracle took place, reported that Jesus was wearing a purple tunic and beneath that, He wore a shirt up to the middle of His chest.

Not only that but those present witnessed three small united hearts in the Blessed Sacrament that represented the Holy Trinity. [19]

---

[19] Galeone, Christine. "7 Amazing Eucharistic Miracles." Beliefnet. (https://www.beliefnet.com/faiths/catholic/7-amazing-eucharistic-miracles.aspx?p=6). January 19, 2019.

The Miracle at Bruges, Belgium

Basilica of the Holy Blood and the Church of Our Lady in Bruges, Belgium contains a vial that contains a drop of the Blood of Christ. The vial was brought there after the second crusade in 1150.

Today, the church offers daily Mass, Eucharistic Adoration, and the procession of the Holy Blood is always held on Ascension Thursday every year. [20]

---

[20] "Bruges, Belgium: Basilica of the Holy Blood and the Church of Our Lady." The Catholic Travel Guide. (https://thecatholictravelguide.com/destinations/belgium/belgium-bruges-basilica-holy-blood/). January 21, 2019.

The Miracle of Cascia, Italy

In 1330, a priest from Siena went to visit a dying farmer.

However, instead of placing the Host in a pyx, he put the Host inside his missal. When he arrived at the man's house, he opened his missal and discovered that the Host was bleeding and the pages were stained with blood. Many investigations concluded that the blood was human blood.

Today, the missal and Host are kept in the lower chapel of the Basilica of St. Rita. [21]

---

[21] "Cascia, Italy: Home of Saint Rita of Cascia and the Eucharistic Miracle of Cascia." The Catholic Traveler Guide. (https://thecatholictravelguide.com/destinations/italy/cascia-italy-home-saint-rita-cascia-eucharistic-miracle-cascia/). January 21, 2019.

Eucharistic Miracle at Herkenrode-Hasselt

On July 25, 1317, a priest from Viversel was called to the home of one of his parishioners who was dying.

The priest sat his handbag on the table while he heard the man's confession.

While the priest was away, one of the family members was curious about the handbag so he carefully inspected it.

The boy pulled out the pyx and opened the cover so see what was inside.

However, as soon as the boy realized that there was a Host inside the pyx, he immediately put everything back inside the bag before anybody saw him.

When the priest returned for his handbag, he reached out for the pyx to give Holy Communion to the sick person.

When the priest opened the pyx, he saw that the Host was bleeding and stuck to the linen that covered the bottom of the pyx. The priest got terrified and immediately take the Host to the Abbey of Herkenrode.

On the way to the Abbey, the priest stopped at a Benedictine monastery.

When he showed the Host to those present, the face of Jesus crowned with thorns appeared inside the Host.

The Host remained in the Abbey of Herkenrode until 1796.

Today, the Host is exposed in Church of St. Quintinus in Hasselt. [22]

---

[22] "Eucharistic Miracle at Herkenrode-Hasselt." The Real Presence. < file:///C:/Users/unsto/AppData/Local/Microsoft/Windows/INetCache/IE/HEZY2ZQ8/Herkenrode.pdf>. July 31, 2019

"Eucharistic Miracle at Herkenrode-Hasselt." Eucharistic Miracles of the World – the Vatican International Exhibition. <https://eucharisticmiraclesoftheworld.weebly.com/belgium.html>. July 31, 2019.

The Eucharistic Miracle of Augsburg, Germany

The Eucharistic Miracle is known as "The Miraculous Good" happened in 1194 in Augsburg, Germany.

In 1194, a devout woman stole a Host after receiving Holy Communion in a handkerchief. The woman took the Blessed Sacrament and placed the Host inside a wax container.

After five years had passed, the woman was being tormented by remorse and confessed her actions to Fr. Berthold, a superior at the convent of Heilig Kreuz.

Fr. Berthold told the woman to return the Host back to church. When the priest opened the wax container, he saw that the Host had transformed into bleeding flesh. The Host was divided into two parts that were connected by the thin threads of the bleeding flesh.

Fr. Berthold immediately showed the Host to the bishop of the city of Udalskalk. The bishop ordered that the Host be transferred to the cathedral in a solemn procession and exhibited in an ostensorium of crystal.

The Host continued to perform many more miracles after this.

One such example was that the Host began to grow and swell up in a phenomenon that lasted from Easter

Sunday all the way until the feast of St. John the Baptist.

After this miracle, Bishop Udalskalk ordered that the Host taken to the convent of the Heilig Kreuz and later proclaimed that in honor of such a miracle, there should be a special commemoration each year in honor of the Eucharistic Miracle.

In 1200, a man named Count Rechber donated a rectangular chest of silver with an opening in the front for the placement of the Blessed Host to the Augustinian Fathers.

Other miracles began to take place shortly after.

On one instance, the Baby Jesus appeared inside the Host dressed in white with a radiant face and a golden crown. On another occasion, a crucifix bleeding. People also witnessed an apparition of Jesus blessing those present.

Today, the Host continues to be exposed in the Convent of the Heileg Kreuz and protected by the Dominican Fathers. [23]

---

[23] "The Guardian Angel: Eucharistic Miracle of Augsburg Germany 1199." Deeper Truth: Catholic Perspectives on Everyday Life. July 22, 2019. (https://www.deepertruthcatholics.com/single-post/2019/07/22/The-Guardian-Angel-Eucharistic-Miracle-of-Augsburg-Germany-1199). July 31, 2019.

The Eucharistic Miracle of Middleburg-Louvain

The Eucharistic Miracle happened in Middleburg when a noblewoman invited her staff to attend Easter Mass. The woman was very devout and focused on her spiritual formation. The woman had hired a new servant, who had not gone to church in many years, a few days before Easter Mass.

When the man, Jan, was about to receive Holy Communion on the tongue, the Host turned into bleeding flesh. Jan removed the Host and the blood began to drip onto the cloth that covered the altar rail.

The priest saw was happened and immediately took the Host with great care and placed the Host in a vessel inside the tabernacle.

The news about the miracle spread and after a careful investigation, the Archbishop approved of the event as an official miracle. [24]

---

[24] "Eucharistic Miracle of Middleburg- Louvain, Belgium 1374." The Eucharist – Jesus is with us. November 19, 2010. <https://eucharistjesuswithus.blogspot.com/2010/11/eucharistic-miracle-of-middleburg.html>. July 31, 2019.

The Miracle at Bois-Seigneur-Isaac

A week before Pentecost in 1405, Jesus began to appear covered in wounds to a man named John of Huldenberg.

On the third apparition, Jesus spoke to John and told him to go to the Chapel of Isaac where Jesus would appear to him next.

The parish priest from the Chapel of Isaac, Fr. Peter Ost, heard Jesus telling him to offer Mass of the Holy Cross in that chapel. The priest obeyed and gathered many people to attend Mass at the chapel.

John of Huldenberg also attended Mass that day, just as Jesus had asked him.

When the priest began to say Mass, he unfolded the corporal where he saw a particle of a Host that had been consecrated the day before. The priest was about to pick up the Host, but the Host began to bleed and clung to the corporal.

The priest jumped back in fear but John comforted the priest telling him that this was a miracle from God and told him about the visions.

The Host continued to bleed for days and after the fourth day, the whole corporal was covered in blood.

Soon after, the blood coagulated and dried up.

Bishop Peter d' Ailly, the bishop of Cambrai, learned about the miracle and began an investigation.

Two years later, the Bishop granted indulgences of forty days to those who visited the chapel at Bois-Seigneur-Isaac, where the corporal was exposed for adoration.

Today, on the Sunday after the Feast of the Birth of Mary, the citizens from Bois-Seigneur-Isaac gather in prayer to honor the Eucharistic Miracle. [25]

---

[25] "Eucharistic Miracle of Bois-Seigneur-Isaac." Eucharistic Miracles of the World - the Vatican International Exhibition.
<file:///C:/Users/unsto/AppData/Local/Microsoft/Windows/INetCache/IE/RVODWQCQ/Boisseigneurisaac.pdf>. July 31, 2019.

The Miracle of Brussels, Belgium

The Eucharistic miracle occurred in 1369 when a merchant from Enghien, who hated Catholics, stole consecrated Hosts.

A few days later, the merchant was mysteriously assassinated. His wife believed that it was a punishment from God for stealing the Hosts. The wife was scared and didn't know what to do so she gave the Hosts to some of her husband's friends. The husband's friends also hated Catholics so they began to slash the Hosts with knives.

The Hosts immediately began to bleed and the men became frightened that they gave the Hosts to a Catholic merchant. The merchant revealed the miracle to the Bishop of Notre Dame, who then took possession of the desecrated Hosts. The bishop took the Hosts in a procession to the Cathedral of St. Gudula. The Duke of Brabant condemned to death the desecrators.

Today, the Hosts are kept in a museum in the Cathedral of St. Gudula. [26]

---

[26] "Eucharistic Miracle of Brussels." The Real Presence. <file:///C:/Users/unsto/AppData/Local/Microsoft/Windows/INetCache/IE/HEZY2ZQ8/Brussels.pdf >. July 31, 2019.

"The Guardian Angel: Two Eucharistic Miracles from Belgium." Deeper Truth: Catholic Perspectives on Everyday Life. August 3, 2016. < https://www.deepertruthcatholics.com/single-post/2016/08/03/The-Guardian-Angel-Two-Eucharistic-Miracles-from-Belgium>. July 31, 2019.

The Miracle of Fiecht

The miracle of Fiecht happened in the village of St. Georgenberg in Fiecht in 1310. One day during a weekly Mass at a church dedicated to George (a holy martyr) and the Holy Apostle James. During Mass, the priest began to have serious doubts about the Eucharist. He found it hard to believe that the wine turned into the actual blood of Christ.

As he was consecrating the wine, it immediately turned into real blood. The blood began to boil and it immediately and the chalice began to overflow as the blood continued running out of the chalice. The abbot, the monks, and the congregation realized that something had happened so they approached the altar to investigate.

The priest was terrified and unable to consume the Precious Blood so the abbot picked up the chalice, along with the cloth that was used to wipe the chalice, and placed it inside the Tabernacle. Soon after this miracle, news broke out throughout the world and many pilgrims began to visit the church to worship the Eucharist and the Precious Blood. The miracle was declared authentic in 1472 when Bishop Georg von Brixen sent the abbot of Wilten, Joahannes Lösch, and the pastors, Sigmund Thaur and Kaspar of Absam to study this phenomenon. [27]

---

[27] "Eucharistic Miracle of Fiecht Austria (1310)." Y Catholic. < https://y-catholic.blogspot.com/>. July 6, 2020.

The Miracle of Ludbreg

The miracle of Ludbreg happened almost the same way as the miracle of Fiecht but with a different outcome.

Just like in Fiecht, a priest had doubts about whether or not the bread and wine turned into the actual Body and Blood of Christ. As he celebrated Mass in 1411 in the chapel of the Count Batthyany's castle, the wine transformed into real Blood at the moment of consecration.

However, unlike in the miracle of Fiecht, the priest was terrified and didn't know what to do. Instead of sharing the miracle, he hired a man to hide the chalice behind the wall of the altar.

The priest asked the man not to tell anybody about this miracle, to which he obliged. The priest himself did not reveal this miracle until he was dying.

As word got out about the chalice and the Precious Blood, people began to make pilgrimages to Ludbreg.

Pope Julius II heard about the miracle and had the chalice brought to Rome but the people of Ludbreg continued to visit the church where the miracle had happened.

In the 18th century, a plague swept in northern Croatia.

The people turned to God for help. When God heard their prayer, they vowed to build a chapel at Ludbreg in honor of this miracle.

However, they weren't able to build the chapel until 1994 when democracy was restored. [28]

---

[28] "The Guardian Angel: Eucharistic Miracle at Ludbreg Croatia, 1411." Deeper Truth: Catholic Perspectives on Everyday Life. 10 February 2020. < https://www.deepertruthcatholics.com/single-post/2020/02/10/The-Guardian-Angel-Eucharistic-Miracle-at-Ludbreg-Croatia-1411>. 7 July 2020.

Exnihilo. "Eucharistic Miracle of Ludbreg Croatia, 1411." Catholictales. 14 September 2018. < https://catholictales.com/eucharistic-miracle-of-ludbreg-croatia-1411/>. 7 July 2020.

The Miracle of Herentals

In 1412, a man named Jan van Langerstede visited the city of Herentals. Jan was a professional thief who visited many churches to steal sacred objects and sell them.

The following day, Jan broke into the church of Porderlee stole the chalice and the ciborium that contained five consecrated Hosts. As he left the city, he was pulled back by a strong but invisible force.

The force kept holding him so in his panic, Jan immediately began to get rid of the Hosts. He tried to get rid of the Hosts by throwing them into a river. But the strong force prevented him from doing so. Jan was in desperation that he hid the Hosts in a place known "De Hegge" and placed them on a big rabbit burrow and ran away.

However, he kept the chalice and ciborium. Soon after, the city judge, Gilbert De Pape, opened an investigation to find out who the criminal was. The police soon found out that Jan was the criminal when they found the chalice and the ciborium hidden in his luggage. Jan was immediately charged and scheduled to hang.

However, after he had already climbed the scaffold, he decided to confess his whole crime to a priest. That was when Jan told the priest about his crime as well as what he had done to the Eucharist.

When the judge heard this, he immediately ordered the execution to be halted in exchange for Jan leading them to the Hosts that he had hidden. Jan escorted the priest, authorities, and other witnesses to the field. When they arrived, they found the Hosts radiating in blinding light and arranged in the form of a cross.

Although it had been a long time since the Hosts were hidden, they were still well preserved and not affected by the weather or anything else. The Hosts were retrieved and they were divided into two groups. Some of the Hosts were taken to Herentals and some to Poederlee in a procession.

The Hosts remained there until the 16th century.

The phenomenon was declared an official miracle by the magistrate of Herentals. Soon after, a small chapel was built in the place where the Hosts were found but later on, it was transformed into a shrine. [29]

---

[29] "The Eucharistic Miracle of Herentals." The Eucharistic Miracles of the World. The Real Presence: Christ in the Eucharist.
<file:///C:/Users/unsto/AppData/Local/Microsoft/Windows/INetCache/IE/RVODWQCQ/Herentals.pdf.>. July 6, 2020.

The Miracle of Morne-Rouge

The Eucharistic Miracle of Morne-Rouge took place on May 8, 1902, on Mount Pelée. On that day, the volcano on the mountain began to erupt lava and ash. The inhabitants of the village immediately ran to the church to ask Our Lady of Deliverance for help. As the ruckus of the volcano approached the church and ran inside the confessionals to seek forgiveness for their sins before their death.

There was no time so the pastor gave a general absolution to those present, distributed Holy Communion, and exposed the Blessed Sacrament for adoration. As they were fervently praying, a woman saw the miracle. She immediately shouted, "The Sacred Heart of Jesus is in the Host!"

Those present also saw Jesus in the Host and saw that He was showing His Sacred Heart that was crowned with thorns. Many people saw Jesus' Precious Blood dripping from His Sacred Heart. The Eucharistic miracle lasted for hours until the priest restored the Host to the Tabernacle. When the volcano stopped erupting, the people found that they were saved from the volcanic lava. [30]

---

[30] Exnihilo. "The Eucharistic Miracle of Morne-Rouge." Catholictales September 17, 2018. < https://catholictales.com/eucharistic-miracle-of-morne-rouge-caribbean-island-martinique-1902/>. July 6, 2020.

The Miracle of Scete

The Miracle of Scete happened somewhere between the 3rd and 4th centuries in Scete, Egypt.

During this time, many men and women followed in the footsteps of St. Anthony the Abbot in a life of prayer and contemplation. Many men joined communal groups, such as monasteries.

One of the monks did not believe that Jesus was present in the Eucharist. Instead, he believed that the Eucharist was a symbol of Jesus. Two other monks approached him quietly and rebuked him for contradicting the church and his blasphemy towards the Eucharist.

However, the monk replied that he would not believe until he saw evidence for himself. The Sunday after this confrontation, the monk was saying Mass when he experienced the Eucharistic miracle. As he was consecrating the bread, the Host on his hands turned into a child.

When the monk raised the Host, an angel appeared with a sword and pierced the boy.

When the monk broke the Host, blood began to flow into the chalice. The Bloodied Host that he held became the Eucharistic bread and he consumed the Host with fervent respect. At Holy Communion, the angel took the Bloodied Particles from the Host and took them to the monks to receive.

After witnessing this miracle, the monk cried out to the Lord telling him that he fully believed that the bread and wine were indeed His Body and Blood. [31]

---

[31] "Eucharistic Miracle of Scete Egypt 3rd Century." Sts With Uns. Our Lady of Lourdes & St. Swithun's. < https://stswithuns.org.uk/eucharistic-miracles-scete>. 7 July 2020.

The Miracle of Herentals

In 1412, a man named Jan van Langerstede visited the city of Herentals. Jan was a professional thief who visited many churches to steal sacred objects and sell them. The following day, Jan broke into the church of Porderlee stole the chalice and the ciborium that contained five consecrated Hosts.

As he left the city, he was pulled back by a strong but invisible force. The force kept holding him so in his panic, Jan immediately began to get rid of the Hosts.

He tried to get rid of the Hosts by throwing them into a river. But the strong force prevented him from doing so. Jan was in desperation that he hid the Hosts in a place known "De Hegge" and placed them on a big rabbit burrow and ran away.

However, he kept the chalice and ciborium.

Soon after, the city judge, Gilbert De Pape, opened an investigation to find out who the criminal was. The police soon found out that Jan was the criminal when they found the chalice and the ciborium hidden in his luggage. Jan was immediately charged and scheduled to hang.

However, after he had already climbed the scaffold, he decided to confess his whole crime to a priest. That was when Jan told the priest about his crime as well as what he had done to the Eucharist.

When the judge heard this, he immediately ordered the execution to be halted in exchange for Jan leading them to the Hosts that he had hidden. Jan escorted the priest, authorities, and other witnesses to the field. When they arrived, they found the Hosts radiating in blinding light and arranged in the form of a cross. Although it had been a long time since the Hosts were hidden, they were still well preserved and not affected by the weather or anything else.

The Hosts were retrieved and they were divided into two groups. Some of the Hosts were taken to Herentals and some to Poederlee in a procession. The Hosts remained there until the 16th century. The phenomenon was declared an official miracle by the magistrate of Herentals. Soon after, a small chapel was built in the place where the Hosts were found but later on, it was transformed into a shrine. [32]

---

[32] "The Eucharistic Miracle of Herentals." The Eucharistic Miracles of the World. The Real Presence: Christ in the Eucharist.
<file:///C:/Users/unsto/AppData/Local/Microsoft/Windows/INetCache/IE/RVODWQCQ/Herentals.pdf.>. July 6, 2020.

The Miracle of Avignon

The miracle of Avignon took place in the Church of the Holy Cross, which is where a Franciscan Order resided.

In the year, 1433, there were terrible storms in the area that caused many floods.

However, by November, the rain had gotten so strong that Sorgue and Rhône Rivers rose. This caused the villagers and the Franciscan Monks to flee.

However, some monks remembered that they had left a Host exposed in the church for Perpetual Adoration.

Therefore, the friar and another monk took a boat to the church to retrieve the Host. The whole town was flooded but after a long trip, the finally reached the church.

When they arrived at the church, they found it that the church was also flooded on the inside.

The monks entered the church thinking that the Host must've been swept away in the water.

However, when they entered, they saw that the church was flooded except for the path that began at the entrance all way up to the altar.

The waters had parted ways the same way that the Red Sea had opened for Moses. The pathway was completely dry and so was the altar so the Host was intact.

Realizing that they had just witnessed a Eucharist Miracle, the monks ordered the rest of the congregation to the church so that they themselves might witness the miracle.

The news spread rapidly and about several hundred people traveled to the church as well so see the miracles for themselves.

Since then, the Franciscan Order holds a feast on the day of the anniversary of the event.[33]

---

[33] "The Eucharistic Miracle of Avignon." The Real Presence in the Eucharist. < file:///C:/Users/unsto/AppData/Local/Microsoft/Windows/INetCache/IE/RVODWQCQ/Avignon1%20(1).pdf>. 7 July 2020.

Exnihilo. "Eucharistic Miracle of Avignon, France – 1433." Catholic Tales. 19 September 2018. < https://catholictales.com/eucharistic-miracle-of-avignon-france-1433/#:~:text=Eucharistic%20Miracle%20of%20Avignon%2C%20France%20%E2%80%93%202014 33.%20The,was%20home%20to%20a%20series%20of%20seven%20popes.>. 7 July 2020.

The Miracle of Dijon

The miracle of Dijon happened in a mischievous way in Monaco in 1430.

A lady had purchased an old monstrance from a man who had surely stolen it since it still contained a consecrated Host inside it. The only time that a Host is placed on a monstrance is for Eucharistic Adoration so chances are that the man must've stolen the monstrance without anybody noticing.

The lady didn't realize that the Host was consecrated or even that the Host was the actual Body of Christ. So the lady got a knife to remove the Host from the monstrance.

However, she accidentally pierced the Host causing the Host to start bleeding. Although the Host began to bleed, the blood quickly dried up and left an image of Jesus seating on a semicircular throne with instruments of His Passion imprinted on the Host.

The lady panicked so she immediately sent the Host to a priest.

From here, the pope, Pope Eugene IV, ordered that the Host be donated to Duke Phillip of Borgogna. The Duke placed the Host in a Basilica in the city of Dijon.

In 1794, the Host remained in the Basilica of Saint Michael the Archangel.

However, the municipality of Dijon seized the Basilica and gave it to a sect that worshipped "la Raison", or the "goddess of reason. Unfortunately, the sect burned the Host and so there wasn't a chapel built to commemorate the Eucharistic Miracle. [34]

---

[34] "1430 Dijon, France." Eucharistic Miracles (1400-1500). The Miracle Hunter. < http://www.miraclehunter.com/eucharistic-miracles/1400-1500.html>. 7 July 2020.

The Miracle of Douai

The miracle at Douai took place on Easter Sunday in 1254 in the Church of St. Amato. The miracle occurred when the parish priest was distributing Holy Communion. The priest accidentally dropped the Host but immediately picked up the consecrated Host.

However, before the priest could pick up the Host, the Host began to float in the air and landed on a purification cloth.

The Host began to glow and the Baby Jesus appeared within the Host. Jesus' apparition was so great that those present could contemplate Him.

The news of the miracle spread throughout and so the Bishop of Cambrai, Thomas de Cantimpré, decided to investigate it for himself. The bishop was skeptical and didn't expect to witness the miracle.

However, when the parish Dean of Church presented the bishop the container where the Host was placed. At first, the bishop didn't see anything miraculous in the Host.

However, the bishop soon saw the face of Christ crowned with thorns with two drops of blood flowing from His forehead within the Host.

Soon, a feast day was made in honor of this miracle every Wednesday of the Holy Week. The Host was conserved and worshipped until the Revolution when the miracle of the Host disappeared.

However, in October 1854, the Pastor of the Church of St. Peter discovered the Host underneath the Altar of the Dead. The Host was still white but the edges were damaged. The priest immediately picked up the Host and placed the Host inside a pyx.[35]

---

[35] "Eucharistic Miracle of Douai, France 1254." The Eucharist - Jesus is With us. 20 November 2010. < https://eucharistjesuswithus.blogspot.com/2010/11/eucharistic-miracle-of-douai-france.html#:~:text=Eucharistic%20Miracle%20of%20Douai%2C%20France%201254.%20Bonum%20universale,unintentionally%20dropped%20a%20consecrated%20Host%20to%20the%20ground. >. 7 July 2020.

The Miracle of Faverney

The miracle at Faverney took place in 1608 in a Benedictine Abbey in Faverney, France.

On the Vigil of the Feast of Pentecost, the monks set up an altar to expose the Host for adoration. Since the lunette of the monstrance was large, the monks decided to place two Hosts inside it. The monks adored the Host up until Vespers when they retired for the day.

However, the monks left the Host exposed all night for those who wished to adore Jesus in the Eucharist.

The next day, the sacristan entered the church and found that it was burning. Most of the church inside had burned – even the altar where the Host was exposed overnight.

The sacristan shouted and called the other monks for help. The other monks responded immediately and quenched the fires.

When the fire was extinguished, the monks searched through the ashes to search for the monstrance, which they thought had been destroyed.

However, they were amazed when they saw that the monstrance was suspended in the air.

The monstrance kept floating in the air and when news broke out about this miracle, people crowded the burned church to see the miracle for themselves. The monks did not know what to do so they asked Capuchin friars of Vesoul for advice. The friars prepared a new altar immediately where the old altar stood and underneath the floating Host.

The friars said Mass and during the elevation of the Host, the miraculous Host descended upon the new altar.

On July 10, Archbishop of Besançon declared that the miracle was authentic. Then Pope Paul V acknowledged the miracle and granted a Bull of Indulgence.

In 1862, the Congregation of Rites authorized the celebration of the miracle, and eventually, the miracle was only honored with a National Eucharistic Congress.

One of the Hosts is still exposed for adoration.

Unfortunately, the other Host was donated to the Church of Dole and finally destroyed by the insurgents and war in 1794. [36]

---

[36] Aaron, Shirley. Eucharistic Miracle Of Faverney, France. Catholics Online. < http://francismary.org/eucharistic-miracle-of-faverney-france/>. 8 July 2020.

The Miracle of La Rochelle

The miracle of La Rochelle was different than the previous miracles. While the other miracles have involved the actual Host showing of Jesus' presence, this one shows Jesus curing through the Eucharist.

On the Easter Sunday of 1461, a woman named, Mrs. Jehan Leclerc, took her twelve-year-old son to the Church of St. Bartholomew.

Her son had been paralyzed and mute since he was seven due to an accidental fall.

When the mother went up to receive Holy Communion, her son signaled to his mother that he also wanted to receive Holy Communion.

However, the pries did not want to give him Holy Communion because the boy hadn't been to confession because he couldn't speak.

However, the boy kept begging and in the end, the priest decided to give him the Blessed Sacrament.

As soon as the child's tongue touched the Host, he began to shake from an invincible force.

Immediately, he healed and was able to move and speak.

The boy shouted out loud, "Adjutorium nostrum in Nomine Domini!" ("Our help is in the name of the Lord!"). [37]

---

[37] "Eucharistic Miracle of La Rochelle." The Eucharistic Miracles of the World. The Real Presence Eucharistic Education and Adoration Association.< http://therealpresence.org/eucharst/mir/engl_mir.htm>. 8 July 2020.

The Miracle of Les Ulmes

The miracle of Les Ulmes happened on June 2, 1668, in the Church of Les Ulmes.

June the second happened to be the Saturday of the Octave of Corpus Christi.

Therefore, the pastor of the church, Nicolas Nezan incense the monstrance.

They began to sing hymn Pange Lingua, and when they reached the stanza 'Verbum Caro Panem Verum,' Jesus appeared in the monstrance replacing the Host.

He a luminous face, had light brown hair that fell over his back, wore a bright white tunic and His hands were crossed over the other.

The apparition of Jesus lasted between 15 minutes to 30 minutes.

His apparition remained when it was on the tabernacle and then when the Host was exposed so that all those present could see the apparition of Jesus.

A few days later, the pastor told his bishop, Bishop Henry Arnauld, who began an investigation.

After many investigations, the miracle was approved and people celebrated the event every anniversary.

In 1901 the International Eucharistic Congress of Angers was celebrated in this parish and in July 1933, during the National Eucharistic Congress, a complete session of the study was dedicated to the miracle of 1668.

However, this miraculous Host was consumed by Vicar of Puy-Notre-Dame out of fear that the Host would be profaned during the French Revolution. [38]

---

[38] Exnihilo. "Eucharistic Miracle of Les Ulmes, France – 1668." Catholic Tales. 11 September 2018. < https://catholictales.com/eucharistic-miracle-of-les-ulmes-france-1668/>. 8 July 2020.

The Miracle of Marseille-En-Beauvais

The miracle of Marseille-En-Beauvais took place in 1533 in a sacrilege way.

One night, a couple of thieves broke into a church and stole a silver ciborium that contained consecrated Hosts. The thieves didn't care about the Hosts so they discarded the consecrated Hosts in a field covered with snow.

The following day, a man named Mr. Jean Moucque found the Hosts while he was walking down the street during a strong snowstorm.

While he was walking, he saw a rock on the side of the road that didn't have any snow on it despite the snowstorm.

Mr. Jean Moucque lifted the rock and found and they were miraculously intact.

He ran and told the church pastor, Father Prothais, and he immediately held a procession to where the Hosts were found.

They gathered the Hosts and respectfully carried the Hosts back to the church.

The people put a cross where the Hosts were found to commemorate the miracle.

However, huge crowds began to form there so they

built a chapel known as "The Chapel of the Sacred Hosts."

Many miracles and healings took place in this chapel: igniting strong devotion to the Blessed Sacrament.

However, the Bishop of Beauvais, Odet de Coligny publicly denounced his faith and converted to Calvinism.

However, before he stepped down, he ordered that the Miraculous Hosts be consumed.

Despite the Miraculous Hosts being gone, the chapel still stands and people celebrate the miracle every year on the second day of January.[39]

"The Guardian Angel: Eucharistic Miracle of Marseille-En-Beauvais, France – 1533. Deeper Truth Blog: Catholic Perspectives on Everyday Life. 17 June 2019. < https://www.deepertruthcatholics.com/single-post/2019/06/17/The-Guardian-AngelEucharistic-Miracle-of-Marseille-En-Beauvais-France---1533>. 9 July 2020.

The Miracle of Paris

The miracle of Paris took place on Easter Sunday on April 2, 1290.

There was a man named Jonathas who hated Catholic Faith and the belief that Jesus was present in the Eucharist.

So on April 2, he was able to steal a consecrated Host with evil intentions. Jonathas really hated everything to do with Catholics so when he got home, he stabbed the Host with a knife.

The Host immediately began to bleed.

The man dropped the Host on a contained and the blood began to fill the container. Jonathas did know what to do so he picked up the Host and threw the Blessed Sacrament in his fireplace.

However, the Host began to float above the flames instead of being consumed by the flames. Jonathas panicked again so he retrieved the Host and threw the Blessed Sacrament into boiling water.

Again, the Host began to float in the air rather than sinking into the boiling water.

Instead, Host took the form of a crucifix.

Jonathas didn't know what else to do so he grabbed the Host and threw the Blessed Sacrament into the bowl of a parishioner of the Church Saint Jean-en–Grève.

The parishioner panicked and immediately ran to the parish priest and gave him the bowl with the Miraculous Host.

The priest placed the Host I a small reliquary in the church of Saint-Jean where people could view the Host there and adore.

The Host remained at the church for centuries.

However, the Host was lost during the French Revolution never to be seen again.

---

[40] "The Guardian Angel: Eucharistic Miracle of Paris, 1290." Deeper Truth Blog: Catholic Perspectives on Everyday Life. 4 January 2017. < https://www.deepertruthcatholics.com/single-post/2017/01/04/The-Guardian-Angel-Eucharistic-Miracle-of-Paris-1290>. 9 July 2020.

The Miracle of Pressac

The miracle of Pressac happened because of a tragedy that took place on Holy Thursday, 1643.

After the priest had celebrated the morning Mass and the congregation had gone to their daily routines, the priest placed the chalice back into the repository.

A veil covered the chalice and two large candles were lit at the foot of the repository.

The repository was right next to an altar dedicated to the Virgin Mary. The altar had four pillars of wood that supported a marble slab that was below a corporal.

After the priest was finished saying Mass and left the church, the sacristan closed the door of the church.

A couple of hours later, people nearby saw thick and black smoke coming from the windows of the church. The windows had been left opened so that probably knocked down the candles and caused the fire.

The people alerted the sacristan and asked him to open the doors to the church.

When they entered the church, they saw that the repository and a painting of the Eucharist were destroyed.

The only thing that was left were the marble slab, corporal, and the foot of the chalice.

The chalice was transformed into a "drops of tin" as it had melted.

The only thing that was left of the chalice was the foot.

However, they noticed that a bubble formed above the destroyed chalice, and above the bubble there was the Host floating above.

The Host remained intact despite the fires and destruction of the chalice.

Instead, the Host had red around the edges.

The vicar, Simon Sauvage, entered the church a few days later and carried the damaged chalice to the main altar for everybody to see.

After the Divine Office of Good Friday, the Host was consumed.[41]

---

[41] "The Guardian Angel: Eucharistic Miracle of Pressac, France, 1643." Deeper Truth Blog: Catholic Perspectives on Everyday Life. 11 January 2017. < https://www.deepertruthcatholics.com/single-post/2017/01/11/The-Guardian-Angel-Eucharistic-Miracle-of-Pressac-France-1643/>. 9 July 2020.

Exnihilo. "Eucharistic Miracle of Pressac, France – 1643." Catholic Tales. 20 September 2018. < https://catholictales.com/eucharistic-miracle-of-pressac-france-1643/>. 9 July 2020.

The Miracle of Ettiswil

The miracle of Ettiswil happened when the devil tried to have a consecrated Host in a Black Mass.

The event happened during the 15th-century Ettiswil, Switzerland when a devil worshipper, Ann Vögtli, stole a consecrated Host from a church.

The woman belonged to a Satanic Sect and was tasked with bringing in the Host to defile it on a Halloween ceremony. Vögtli ran all the way to the cemetery but when she reached the wall, she wasn't able to pass.

The Host became too heavy and soon.

She was not able to enter the cemetery or even return. Panicking, she threw the Host close to a fence in the nettles.

The following morning, a young lady discovered the Eucharist floating above the nettles.

However, the Host had been divided into seven sections and took the form of a flower. One section settled in the middle while the other six sections formed into pedals. Not only that, but there was a very luminous light surrounded the rose-like Hosts.

The lady did not touch the Hosts but instead, she ran and informed the parish priest about the miracle.

The priest arrived and tried to pick up the Hosts to take them to church.

However, he wasn't able to remove the section that was in the middle.

The priest saw this as a sign that a chapel should be built there.

Once the chapel was built, the priest put the seventh section of the Host inside a relic and placed the relic in the chapel for perpetual adoration.

Since then, many miracles and healings have taken place.[42]

---

[42] "Eucharistic Miracle: You Won't Believe What Happened When a Satanic Follower Tried to Steal the Eucharist." Catholic FB. 21 November 2017. < https://www.catholicfb.com/wont-believe-happened-satanic-follower-tried-steal-eucharist/>. 9 July 2020.

Kosloski, Philip. "When a satanic follower tried to steal the Eucharist." Aleteia 24 October 2017. < https://aleteia.org/2017/10/24/when-a-satanic-follower-tried-to-steal-the-eucharist/>. 9 July 2020.

The Miracle of Saint-André

The miracle of Saint-André took place on January 26, 1902, in a French Colony known as La Réunion.

Abbot Henry Lacombe, the pastor in the church of Saint-André, was celebrating perpetual adoration. The Blessed Sacrament was exposed in the tabernacle above the altar where the priest was saying Mass.

After the priest elevated the Host and began praying the "Our Father," the priest looked up at the Host and saw a bright halo around the rays of the monstrance.

Despite the miracle, the priest tried earnestly to continue saying Mass.

When it was time for Holy Communion, the priest looked up at the monstrance but this time he saw Jesus' face. Jesus' eyes were lowered and a crown of thorns on His forehead.

The priest saw that Jesus had a facial expression of extreme suffering. The priest fought back the tears and continued to say Mass.

After Mass, the priest returned to the sacristy and called the older children from the choir to approach the altar and look carefully at the monstrance.

The children returned to the priest and reported that they had seen Jesus' face in the Host.

The priest called a college student to look at the Eucharist but didn't tell him anything else. The student obeyed and did as he was asked.

However, the student immediately returned and excitedly exclaimed that he saw Jesus' face in the Host.

As news of this miracle spread, people from all places and different social statuses went to the church to see the miracle for themselves.

Jesus' sorrowful expression turned into a joyous face and the crown of thorns disappears. Jesus' face disappeared and a crucifix appeared from top to bottom.

After the Eucharistic blessing and the recital of the Tantum Ergo, the vision disappeared." [43]

---

[43] "Eucharistic Miracles (1900-2000)." The Miracle Hunter. < http://www.miraclehunter.com/eucharistic-miracles/1900-2000.html>. 9 July 2020.

"The Guardian Angel: Eucharistic Miracle of Saint Andre ISLAND OF LA RÉUNION, 1902." Deeper Truth Blog: Catholic Perspectives on Everyday Life. 14 March 2018. < https://www.deepertruthcatholics.com/single-post/2018/03/14/The-Guardian-AngelEucharistic-Miracle-of-Saint-Andre-ISLAND-OF-LA-R%C3%89UNION-1902>. 9 July 2020.

The Miracles of Benningen

The miracles of Benningen happened because of a feud between two neighbors.

In 1216, there were two millers who had hated each other for many years.

Soon they had reached the boiling point so one of them got an idea to frame his enemy with the worst crime ever. One of them went to church and received Holy Communion.

However, instead of consuming the Host, he took the Blessed Sacrament and hid the Host among the stones of the mill that his rival owned. His intent was to frame him and make him look like a villainous blasphemer.

However, the Host began to bleed a few days later on the Feast of St. Gregory. The Host bled profusely and caught the attention of the villagers and the Bishop.

After the news of the miracle spread, the thief felt an extreme sense of guilt that he repented and confessed his sin. The Host was retrieved and a chapel was built in that area.

The Bishop of Augsburg, Frederich, placed the Host into a prized container.in the Church of St. Martin in Memmingen.

Unfortunately, the prized container and the Host disappeared.

Two other miracles took place in this area.

In 1222, a priest was saying Mass. When the time for the consecration took place and the priest raised the Host, the Host began to drip blood. There was so much blood that the corporal was stained.

Another miracle took place in 1465.

In this case, a farmer broke into a church that was burning to save the relic of the miracle. The whole church was destroyed but in 1938, Pope Pius XI constructed a basilica to replace the ruins.

Today, many people go to Meerssen every year to venerate the relic of the miracle. [44]

---

[44] "Eucharistic Miracle of Benningen." The Eucharistic Miracles of the World. The Real Presence. Christ in the Eucharist. <http://therealpresence.org/eucharst/mir/english_pdf/Benningenn.pdf>. 9 July 2020.

"Eucharistic Miracle of Benningen, Germany 1216 and 1465." Our Lady of Lourdes & St Swithun's. < https://stswithuns.org.uk/eucharistic-miracles-of-benningen-germany>. 9 July 2020.

The Miracle of Bettbrunn

The miracle of Bettbrunn happened because of a very pious man from the village of Bettbrunn wanted to adore the Blessed Sacrament every day.

In 1125, a farmer was deeply devoted to the Blessed Sacrament but lived an hour and a half from the closest church, the Church of Tholling, so it was hard for him to go to church daily. Therefore, he decided to steal a Host the next time he went to church.

The farmer placed the Host inside a walking stick. The man made an opening on the top of the stick and placed the Host in there. The man took the walking stick with him every day when he tended to his herd.

Whenever he could, he would take a break to pray. He would stick his walking stick on the ground and knelt down to adore Christ in the Eucharist for many hours. The man continued his routine of walking his herd and praying before the Blessed Sacrament for many months.

However, one day, he got frustrated when his herd was straying too far.

Without thinking, the man threw the stick at his cattle. When the stick hit the ground, the Host fell out of the stick.

With deep remorse, he ran towards the Blessed Sacrament to pick up the Host.

However, he was unable to lift the Host.

After many attempts, he decided to go to the parish priest of Tholling to tell him what had happened. The priest followed the farmer but he was also unable to lift up the Host.

Soon, the priest called for the Bishop Hartwich of Regensburg for help. The bishop, along with all his clergymen, went to the location.

However, the bishop wasn't able to lift the Host either. But when he promised to build a chapel in that area was he able to finally lift the Host.

The chapel was completed in 1125 and the precious relic was placed there. Unfortunately, a fire broke out in 1330 and destroyed the church. The chapel was rebuilt and one of the pillars from the previous church was placed in the interior.[45]

---

[45] "Eucharistic Miracle of Bettbrunn." The Eucharistic Miracles of the World. The Real Presence. Christ in the Eucharist. < http://therealpresence.org/eucharst/mir/english_pdf/Bettbrunn.pdf>. 9 July 2020.

The Miracle of Erding

The miracle of Erding happened because of a poor and ignorant peasant. In the 17th century, there was a poor farmer living in Erding, Germany.

Although he worked hard and long hours, he wasn't able to compete with his neighbor who was also a farmer but much wealthier. So the farmer asked his neighbor for advice and how he was able to be so wealthy.

The neighbor answered that he owed his success to the Holy Eucharist. His neighbor explained that he had the Holy Eucharist in his house.

However, what he really meant was that he lived in contemplation and adoration to the Blessed Sacrament so he always had the Holy Eucharist in his heart.

The farmer did not understand what his neighbor meant. He thought that his neighbor meant that he had an actual Host in his house so he decided to steal and Host and use the Blessed Sacrament as some kind of object that would bring him luck. So the farmer went to Mass on a Holy Thursday and when he received communion, he hid the Host in a clean linen and left the church. Even though the farmer didn't know much about the faith and what the Blessed Sacrament really was, he began to feel guilt and decided to return to the church and tell the priest what he had done.

Jesus in the Eucharistic

However, as he was walking back, the Host slipped from his hand and disappeared in the air. The man searched and searched but couldn't find the Host. Afraid of what had happened, he rushed to the priest and confessed what he had done.

The priest immediately went with the man to where he had lost the Host. When they arrived, the priest found the Host. The Host was resting on a pile of dirt but the Host was emitting a bright blinding light.

The priest tried picking up the Host, but the Host flew up in the air and disappeared. The priest was frightened by what he saw so he alerted the Bishop and informed him about the situation. So the bishop, along with the villagers who heard about the miracle went up to where the miracle had taken place.

The bishop also found the Host illuminating the bright light and resting on a pile of dirt. The bishop bent over to pick up the Host, but the Host flew up in the air and disappeared forever. The bishop decided to build a chapel in that location to honor the Eucharistic Miracle that had taken place.

Over the years, many pilgrims made their way to that location to also worship the Blessed Sacrament.

However, the chapel was too small to fit the crowds so in 1675 the local authorities constructed a bigger church.

Two years later on September 19, 1677, Bishop Kaspar Kunner of Freising blessed the new church and dedicated it to the Most Precious Blood.

Many other relics were brought to the church, such as the Most Precious Blood of Christ.

Today, the church is under the care of the monks of St. Paul of the Desert.[46]

---

[46] "The story of the Eucharistic Miracle of Erding." *Erding, Germany: Eucharistic Miracle.* The Catholic Travel Guide. < https://thecatholictravelguide.com/destinations/germany/erding-germany-eucharistic-miracle/>. 10 July 2020.

The Miracle of Kranenburg

The miracle of Kranenburg took place in 1280 when a shepherd of Kranenburg was very ill. One day, he went to Mass and received Holy Communion.

However, the man suffered from an illness that prevented him from swallowing the Host.

On his way home, he couldn't take it anymore so he spit out the Host and threw the Blessed Sacrament against a tree in his garden. The man felt extreme remorse because of what he had done so he decided to confess to the priest about his sacrilege. The priest immediately followed the man to where he had thrown the Eucharist.

However, they were unable to find the Host and after a long time they gave up.

Years passed and the man couldn't forget what he had done so he decided to cut down the tree. As he was cutting the tree in half, he found a perfectly carved crucifix inside the tree.

The man immediately ran to the priest to tell him what had happened. Soon, news of the event spread, and the Bishops of Cologne and the Count of Kiev decided to investigate the phenomenon.

Meanwhile, pilgrims from all over began to flock at the site.

In 1408, the town's people began to construct a church in honor of the Eucharistic Miracle.

This miracle was so great that popes and bishops promoted the adoration of the Miraculous Crucifix and granted many privileges and indulgences to those who venerated and honored the Miraculous Crucifix. [47]

---

[47] "Eucharistic Miracle of Kraneburg, District of Kleve." The Eucharistic Miracles of the World. The Real Presence. Christ in the Eucharist.
<http://therealpresence.org/eucharst/mir/english_pdf/Kranenburg.pdf>. 10 July 2020.

The Miracle of Regensburg

The miracle of Regensburg happened in two different events that go hand in hand with each other. On Holy Thursday on March 25, 1255, a priest was taking Holy Communion to a dying man.

However, when he entered the city, he found himself in front of a river that was overflowing because of a storm from the previous day.

To pass to the other side, the people had placed a plank of wood. Unfortunately, the priest slipped and dropped the ciborium that contained the Blessed Sacrament. The priest felt extreme guilt and when the people found out about the accident, they decided to build a chapel there as an act of reparation.

On September 8, 1255, Bishop Albert consecrated the chapel in honor of the Savior, to which the Holy Eucharist was carried in a solemn procession. Ever since the chapel was built, there have been many miracles that have taken place there.

The second miracle happened two years later when a priest was celebrating Mass in that chapel. The priest had doubts about whether or not Jesus was really in the Eucharist.

During the consecration, the priest elevated the chalice when he heard a noise coming from the altar. The man saw that the Jesus from the crucifix was extending his arms towards the priest.

Jesus then took the chalice from the priest and exhibited the Precious Blood so that the faithful could adore Him.

The priest felt a great sense of guilt and felt to his knees begging Jesus to forgive him for doubting His presence in the Holy Eucharist. As a sign of forgiveness, Jesus returned the chalice back to the priest.

The miraculous crucifix is still preserved in the town of Regensburg where many pilgrims visit and worship Jesus in honor of the miracle. [48]

---

[48] "The Guardian Angel: The Eucharistic Miracle of Regensburg." Deeper Truth Blog: Catholic Perspectives on Everyday Life. 12 December 2018. < https://www.deepertruthcatholics.com/single-post/2018/12/12/The-Guardian-Angel-The-Eucharistic-Miracle-of-Regensburg>. 10 July 10, 2020.

The Miracle of Walldürn

The miracle of Walldürn happened in 1330 when a priest, Fr. Heinrich Otto, was saying Mass.

As soon as he had finished the consecration, he placed the chalice on the altar but accidentally knocked it off spilling the Precious Blood on the altar cloth. The Precious Blood immediately took the image of Jesus Christ crucified with eleven thorn-crowned heads surrounding it.

Fr. Heinrich was afraid because he thought that he had committed a sacrilege by spilling the Precious Blood.

Afraid of what had happened, Fr. Heinrich hid the cloth under the altar in a secure place.

Fr. Heinrich kept this secret to himself until his death when he revealed it to his confessor. The corporal with the Precious Blood was found immediately and enshrined.

News spread of this miracle and thousands of pilgrims traveled to the church in Walldürn to view the Holy Corporal.

This Eucharistic Miracle produced many healings, miracles, and conversions.

In 1445, Pope Eugene IV officially recognized this event as an official miracle and had a church built there.

In 1962, Pope John XXIII promoted the church into a minor basilica.

The basilica is known as the Minor Basilica of Saint George and the Most Precious Blood. "Walldurn, Germany: Home to the Eucharistic Miracle of Walldurn."[49]

---

[49] "Walldurn, Germany: Home to the Eucharistic Miracle of Walldurn." The Catholic Travel Guide. < https://thecatholictravelguide.com/destinations/germany/walldurn-germany-home-eucharistic-miracle-walldurn/>. 10 July 2020.

The Miracle of Wilsnack

The miracle of Wilsnack took place in August 1383 in Wilsnack when it was attacked by Count Heinrich von Bulow. The village and the church were robbed and set on fire.

However, despite the church being burned down, the priest found three perfectly intact Hosts, which were bleeding.

Soon, many miracles began to take place where the three Hosts were not being kept for adoration.

One popular healing was that of Count Dietrich von Wenckstern. The Count had doubts about the Eucharist and wondered if Jesus was really present.

Soon, the Count lost his vision but regained it as soon as he repented for disbelieving.

In 1384, the Bishop of Havelburg had confirmed the miracle of the "Bleeding" Hosts of Wilsnack as an authentic miracle.

Pope Urban VI, the Archbishop of Magdeburg, and of the Bishops of Brandenburg, Havelberg, pilgrims, and Levus all contributed to the construction of a church, Church of St. Nikolai, to venerate the Eucharistic Miracle.

Unfortunately, there was another fire in 1522 and the monstrance that contained the relics of the three Hosts was destroyed. [50]

---

[50] "Eucharistic Miracles (1300-1400)." The Miracle Hunter. <http://www.miraclehunter.com/eucharistic-miracles/1300-1400.html>. 10 July 2020.

The Miracles of Altari

The miracle of Altari, Italy happened when a sorceress tricked a woman into committing a sacrilege.

In the 13th century, there was a woman who had lost her love. She was desperate and would do anything possible to get back her lover.

After trying to win back his love in vain, she decided to take drastic measures. Therefore, the woman went to see a sorceress to get a love potion from her. The sorceress accepted to help her make a love potion.

However, the sorceress told the woman to steal the Blessed Sacrament to use it in the potion.

The woman agreed so she went to church to commit her crime.

The following day, the woman went to Mass and received Holy Communion. Instead of consuming the Host, she secretly spit out the Blessed Sacrament and placed the Host in a cloth.

The woman kept the Host in the cloth until she was able to go back to the sorceress. After three days, the woman took out the cloth to check up on the Blessed Sacrament.

However, the Host had transformed into real flesh that was bleeding.

She realized that the Host she had stolen had taken the physical appearance of Jesus. The woman immediately ran to the church to confess what she had done.

When the sorceress heard what had happened, she repented for her part in her crime and converted to Christianity.

Pope Gregory IX investigated the event and declared the phenomenon to be an actual Eucharistic Miracle.

The Host remains today in Cathedral of Altari where the Host is on display in a monstrance. [51]

---

[51] Kosloski, Philip. "When a Woman Stole the Eucharist to Make a Love Potion." Spirituality. Aletia. 21 February 2018. < https://aleteia.org/2018/02/21/when-a-woman-stole-the-eucharist-to-make-a-love-potion/>. 7 July 10, 2020.

"Deeper truth: Eucharistic Miracle of Alatri, Italy, 1228. Deeper Truth. <https://www.blogtalkradio.com/deeper-truth/2019/09/24/deepertruth-eucharistic-miracle-of-alatri-italy-1228>. 10 July 2020.

The Miracles of Asti of 1535

The miracle of Asti on July 25, 1535, while Fr. Domenico Occelli celebrated Mass at the Collegiate Church. During the consecration, Fr. Domenico was beginning to break the Host in half. However, as the priest was breaking the Host, he noticed that along with the breaking of the Host blood began to flow. Three drops of blood fell into the chalice and the fourth one remained at the bottom of the Host. The priest decided to continue Mass but when he completely broke the Host in half, blood began to pour out. The priest was scared and couldn't believe what he was seeing so he asked those present to approach the altar and see the miracle for themselves.

After the people had seen the miracle, the priest decided to continue saying Mass. When the priest was about to consume the Host, the blood disappeared immediately and the Host returned to its normal state. The church officials investigated the event and when it was certified as an official Eucharistic Miracle, Pope Paul III granted indulgences to those who visited the Saint's church on the anniversary of the miracle along with the reciting of three "Our Fathers" and three "Hail Marys." [52]

---

[52] "The Guardian Angel: Eucharistic Miracle of Asti, 1535." Deeper Truth Blog: Catholic Perspectives on Everyday Life. 2 May 2018. < https://www.deepertruthcatholics.com/single-post/2018/05/02/The-Guardian-Angel-Eucharistic-Miracle-of-Asti-1535>. 10 July 2020.

"Eucharistic Miracle of Asti." The Eucharistic Miracles of the World. The Real Presence: Christ in the Eucharist. < http://therealpresence.org/eucharst/mir/english_pdf/Asti1.pdf>. 10 July 2020.

The Miracles of Asti of 1718

The miracle of Asti took place on May 10, 1718, when Father Francesco Scotto was saying Mass at the Opera Milliavacca. When the priest was about to elevate the Host to consecrate it into the Blessed Sacrament, a doctor, Dr. Ambrogio, realized that the Host that the priest was using was broken into two parts. The doctor thought that if the Host was broken, then it wouldn't be transformed into the Body of Christ. So as soon as the priest elevated the chalice, the doctor ran to the sacristy to retrieve another consecrated Host. While the doctor was retrieving a new Host, the priest elevated the Host and realized that the two parts were tainted by blood, the bottom of the chalice had blood, as well as the corporal. At the same time, the doctor arrived with the new consecrated Host.

However, he realized that the Host that the priest was holding was bleeding and began to cry. The people attending Mass also saw the miracle for themselves. Many other doctors, priests, professors, and other highly educated people also witnessed the miracle and confirmed its authenticity. Another thing that confirmed the miracle was the chalice that contained the bloodstains. Written testimonies were kept in the Opera Pia Milliavacca along with the chalice and the consecrated Host. [53]

---

[53] "Eucharistic Miracle of Asti." The Eucharistic Miracles of the World. The Real Presence: Christ in the Eucharist. < http://therealpresence.org/eucharst/mir/english_pdf/Asti2.pdf>. 10 July 2020.

The Miracle of Bagno di Romagna

The miracle of Bagno di Romagna, also known as "Holy Cloth Soaked by Blood," in 1412. The miracle took place in the Camaldolese Abbey of Santa while a priest was saying Mass. The priest was having doubts about Jesus' real presence in the Eucharist. During the consecration, the priest looked at the chalice and saw that the blood was flowing out of the chalice and into the corporal. The priest felt ashamed that he doubted Jesus' real presence in the Eucharist. The priest began to weep profoundly and told the people in the church about his disbelief. He then asked the people to approach the altar to see the miracle for themselves.

In 1958, His Excellency Domenico Bornigia wanted to medically verify that the bloodstains were actual human blood so he ordered a chemical analysis to be done at the University of Florence. The results came back positive as being real human blood. Since then, the corporal is carried in procession every year on the Feast of Corpus Christi and is exposed every Sunday of the temperate season which lasts from March to November. Today, the relic of the Eucharistic Miracle is kept in the Basilica of St. Mary Assumed. [54]

---

[54] "The Eucharistic Miracles of North-Central Italy." Italia: Agenzia Nazionale Turismo. < http://www.italia.it/en/travel-ideas/religion-and-spirituality/the-italy-of-eucharistic-miracles/the-eucharistic-miracles-of-north-central-italy.html>. 11 July 10, 2020.

Ryan, Stephen. "There are 22 Eucharistic Miracles in Italy. The Powerful Sign of God on our 'Distracted' Nation." Mystic Post. 23 May 2018. < https://mysticpost.com/2018/05/oolthere-are-22-eucharistic-miracles-in-italy-the-powerful-sign-of-god-on-our-distracted-nation/>. 11 July 2020.

The Miracle of Cava dei Tirreni

The miracle of Cava Dei Tirreni happened during a terrible plague in Naples in May 1656.

During 1656, a deadly epidemic hit Naples as the Spanish troops from Sardinia. The Spanish were conquering all territories fast and violently so the epidemic spread along with their activity. The pandemic was so terrible that thousands of victims caught the virus and died.

Fr. Paolo Franco was one of a few priests who did not contract the virus. Fr. Paolo was divinely inspired to lead the people in a procession of reparation to stop the pandemic. Despite the dangerous rate of infection, the priest led the people in the procession of reparation a few miles away from the summit of the Castello. When they arrived at the mountain, Fr. Paolo took the Blessed Sacrament and blessed the people.

The people were immediately healed and the pandemic stopped.[55]

---

[55] "The Eucharistic Miracle of Cava Dei Tirreni." The Eucharistic Miracles of the World. The Real Presence: Christ in the Eucharist. <http://therealpresence.org/eucharst/mir/english_pdf/Cavadeitirreni.pdf>. 1 July 2020.

The Miracle of Dronero

The miracle of Dronero happened on Sunday, August 3, 1631, when a great fire broke out in the town of Dronero in the Marquisate of Saluzzo.

The people tried everything they could to quench the fire, but the fire was too strong to control. The fire continued to consume the town and there was no way to stop it. At the moment, Fr. Maurizio da Ceva was divinely inspired to bless the fire with the Most Blessed Sacrament. The priest organized a group of people to go in a procession with the Blessed Sacrament to where the fire was at its worst. As the sun was, the priest and the congregation reach the fire and lifted the Blessed Sacrament and the fire stopped at once.

Since then, the citizens of Dronero gather every year on the occasion of the feast of Corpus Domini to honor the miracle in a procession with the Most Blessed Sacrament.[56]

---

[56] "Dronero (Cuneo), 1631." There are 22 Eucharistic Miracles in Italy. The Powerful Sign of God on our 'Distracted' Nation. Mystic Post. < https://mysticpost.com/2018/05/oolthere-are-22-eucharistic-miracles-in-italy-the-powerful-sign-of-god-on-our-distracted-nation/>. 11 July 2020.

The Miracle of Ferrara

The Eucharistic Miracle of Ferrara occurred in the Basilica of Santa Maria in Vado. On an Easter Sunday, Fr. Pietro da Verona, Prior of the Basilica, was celebrating Mass of Resurrection. During the consecration, the priest broke the Host in half and a stream of blood immediately gushed and the droplets stained the small vault over the altar of the celebration. Those who attended Mass claim that they also saw the Host taking a red color and the figure of a baby inside the Host. Bishop Amato of Ferrara and Archbishop Gherardo of Ravenna investigated the miracle. They saw the Blood, still fresh, staining the ceiling.

News of the event spread and the church became a pilgrim destination. The pilgrims were so great that in 1495, Duke Ercole d'Este had the church renovated and enlarged. However, the blood-stained small vault was later enclosed in a small temple built in 1595 and is still visible today in the monumental Basilica of S. Maria in Vado. [57]

---

[57]

"Ferrara, 1171." There are 22 Eucharistic Miracles in Italy. The Powerful Sign of God on our 'Distracted' Nation. Mystic Post. < https://mysticpost.com/2018/05/oolthere-are-22-eucharistic-miracles-in-italy-the-powerful-sign-of-god-on-our-distracted-nation/>. 11 July 2020.

"The Eucharistic Miracles of North-Central Italy." Agenzia Nazionale Turismo. <http://www.italia.it/en/travel-ideas/religion-and-spirituality/the-italy-of-eucharistic-miracles/the-eucharistic-miracles-of-north-central-italy.html>. 12 July 12, 2020.

The Miracles of Florence

There were two Eucharistic Miracle that took place in Florence on two separate occasions.

The first miracle took place in the Church of Sant'Ambrogio. After a priest finished celebrating Mass, he didn't realize that he had left a few drops of Precious Blood in the chalice. The following day, as he was preparing to say Mass, he took out the chalice and found drops of living, raw, and incarnated blood inside it.

The priest showed this miracle to all the women of the monastery, the townspeople, clergy, and the bishop. He immediately collected the Precious Blood in a crystal ampoule. The priest placed the Precious Blood for the public to view and adore.

When the Bishop, Ardingo, of Pavia heard about the miracle, he ordered the relic be taken to him. The bishop kept the Precious Blood for several weeks but returned the Precious Blood back to the convent near the Church of Sant'Ambrogio. The crystal container with the Precious Blood was placed in a white marble tabernacle that was constructed specifically for this miracle.

In 1399, Pope Boniface IX granted those who visited the Church of Sant'Ambrogio and adored the Precious Blood.

The second miracle took place on Good Friday in 1595. The event began when a candle from the altar fell to the ground and began a fire. Those present approached the altar to turn off the fire and save the Blessed Sacrament and chalice. However, in all the commotion, six fragments of the consecrated Host fell from the pyx and onto the burning carpet. However, despite falling into the fire, the fragments were intact and all joined into one fragment.

In 1628, Archbishop Marzio Medici of Florence had the Host investigated and found that the Hosts were still incorrupt. To venerate the Miraculous Host, he placed a precious reliquary for the Hosts to be kept on.

Since then, the people visit the church every May during the Forty Hours Devotion to adore and honor the Miraculous Host.[58]

---

[58] "Florence, 1292 and 1595." There are 22 Eucharistic Miracles in Italy. The Powerful Sign of God on our 'Distracted' Nation. Mystic Post. < https://mysticpost.com/2018/05/oolthere-are-22-eucharistic-miracles-in-italy-the-powerful-sign-of-god-on-our-distracted-nation/>. 11 July 2020.

The Miracle of Turin

The Eucharistic Miracle of Turin happened in 1453 during a war between the army of Renato d'Angiò against the militia of the Duke Lodovico di Savoia. The fight took place in the Alta Val Susa near Exilles. After this fight ended, the soldiers began looting the village. Foolishly, some of them entered the church and began stripping any valuables they could find. One of them broke the door of the tabernacle and stole the monstrance with the consecrated Hosts. The soldier wrapped up everything he could find and stocked them on the back on his mule. As he was passing by the Church of the Holy Spirit, his mule stumbled and fell. The sack opened and the monstrance fell out.

However, the monstrance began to rise above the houses and other buildings. The people came out and contemplated the miracle with profound amazement. The bishop was informed immediately about the miracle and ran to see the miracle for himself. The bishop took a cup with him and when he reached the site of the miracle, he raised the cup upwards. The consecrated Hosts carefully descended and placed themselves in the cup. [59]

---

[59] "The Eucharistic Miracles of North-Central Italy." Agenzia Nazionale Turismo. <http://www.italia.it/en/travel-ideas/religion-and-spirituality/the-italy-of-eucharistic-miracles/the-eucharistic-miracles-of-north-central-italy.html>. 12 July 12, 2020.

"Turin, 1453." There are 22 Eucharistic Miracles in Italy. The Powerful Sign of God on our 'Distracted' Nation. Mystic Post. < https://mysticpost.com/2018/05/oolthere-are-22-eucharistic-miracles-in-italy-the-powerful-sign-of-god-on-our-distracted-nation/>. 11 July 2020.

The Miracle of Gruaro

The Eucharistic Miracle happened in Gruaro in 1294. One day, a young woman went to the public washhouse along the Versiola canal. The woman was washing the altar linens of the Church of St. Giusto. As the woman was washing the linen, she noticed that the linens were covered in blood. She took them out of the water to investigate to see where the blood was coming from.

When she unfolded the linens, she saw a consecrated Host lost in the pile. The Host had remained there by mistake so when the woman realized what was happening, she immediately ran to alert the pastor who in turn alerted Bishop of Concordia, Giacomo di Ottonello from Cividade.

As soon as the bishop heard about the miracle, he asked that the cloth be taken to his Cathedral in Concordia.

However, the pastor of Gruaro and the family of the Counts of Valvasone, patrons of the churches of Gruaro and of Valvasone, also wanted to keep the cloth. The bishop and the Counts couldn't agree on who could keep it so they asked the Pope for help.

After both sides were heard, the pope let the Counts keep the relic on a condition that they build a church dedicated to the Most Holy Body of Christ and place the relic there.

The church was completed in 1483 and since then, the relic has been kept there.[60]

---

[60] "Gruaro (Venice), 1294." There are 22 Eucharistic Miracles in Italy. The Powerful Sign of God on our 'Distracted' Nation. Mystic Post. < https://mysticpost.com/2018/05/oolthere-are-22-eucharistic-miracles-in-italy-the-powerful-sign-of-god-on-our-distracted-nation/>. 11 July 2020.

"The Eucharistic Miracles of North-Central Italy." Agenzia Nazionale Turismo. <http://www.italia.it/en/travel-ideas/religion-and-spirituality/the-italy-of-eucharistic-miracles/the-eucharistic-miracles-of-north-central-italy.html>. 12 July 12, 2020.

The Miracle of Macerata

The Eucharistic Miracle of Macerata occurred when a priest was celebrating Mass. The priest was pious but he sometimes wondered whether Jesus was really present in the Eucharist.

Unfortunately, the priest was having these doubts during Mass so when he was consecrating the Host, he broke the Host and blood began to fall from the Host and fall onto the corporal and chalice.

The priest immediately told Bishop Nicholas of San Martino about the miracle. The bishop ordered that the relic be taken to the cathedral.

Today, the relic is exposed in the Cathedral of Holy Mary Assumed and St. Giuliano, and under the altar of the Most Holy Sacrament. [61]

---

[61] "Macerata, 1356" There are 22 Eucharistic Miracles in Italy. The Powerful Sign of God on our 'Distracted' Nation. Mystic Post. < https://mysticpost.com/2018/05/oolthere-are-22-eucharistic-miracles-in-italy-the-powerful-sign-of-god-on-our-distracted-nation/>. 11 July 2020.

The Miracle of Rimini

The Eucharistic Miracle of Rimini took place in 1223 when St. Anthony was challenged about the true presence of Jesus in the Eucharist.

A heretic named Bonovillo didn't believe in the power of the Eucharist and wanted to prove to everybody that the Eucharist was just a lie. Therefore, he set up a time for the challenge to take place in the Piazza Grande in front of a large audience.

The challenge involved a mule to see if the mule could recognize Jesus in the Eucharist. The man challenged St. Anthony exclaiming, "'Father! I tell you before all these people: I will believe in the Eucharist if my mule, after fasting for three days, adores the Host which you offer him rather than eating the fodder which I give him.'"

Therefore, he stopped feeding his mule for a few days so that he was in a state of starvation. So the heretic took the mule to the plaza and placed it in front of St. Anthony and the crowd.

He also took food for the mule to make it choose which one was greater. He imagined that the mule would ignore the Blessed Sacrament and go for the food instead.

So the heretic placed some food on one side while St. Anthony was on the other side.

At the same time, St. Anthony approached the mule with a consecrated Host inside.

St. Anthony told the mule, "'In virtue and in the name of your
Creator, Who I, as unworthy as I am, hold in my hands, I tell and order you:

Come forward immediately and render homage to the Lord with all due respect so that heretics and evildoers will understand that all creatures must humble themselves before their Creator whom priests hold in their hands at the altar.'"

The mule refused the food and instead, it approached St. Anthony. The mule bent its front legs before the Blessed Sacrament and remained down in adoration. The heretic was embarrassed and those who were present were amazed at the majesty of the Eucharist and how Jesus is really present. To commemorate this miracle, a small church was built and dedicated to St Anthony in the Piazza Tre Martiri. [62]

---

[62] "There are 22 Eucharistic Miracles in Italy. The Powerful Sign of God on our 'Distracted' Nation." Mystic Post. 23 May 2018. <https://mysticpost.com/2018/05/oolthere-are-22-eucharistic-miracles-in-italy-the-powerful-sign-of-god-on-our-distracted-nation/>. 13 July 2020.

The Miracle of Mogoro

The miracle of Mogoro took place on the Italian island of Sardinia the day after Easter in 1604.

On this day, Father Salvatore Spiga, the pastor of the church of Saint Bernard, was celebrating Mass. While he was distributing Holy Communion, two men approached him to receive Holy Communion. These two men lived lives of crime and sin. Nevertheless, the priest gave them Holy Communion.

However, as soon as they received Communion, the man spit out the Blessed Sacrament onto the floor below the altar rail. The men claimed that the Hosts became hot as burning embers that were burning their tongues.

The men felt an extreme sense of remorse since they had repented from their sins before receiving the Blessed Eucharist.

The men were ashamed and embarrassed that they ran away from the church.

The priest bent down to pick up the fallen Hosts.

However, when he lifted up the Hosts, he saw that the Hosts had left imprints on the stone as if they had been sculpted.

The priest tried to wash the stone to remove the imprints but was unsuccessful.

A notary, Pedro Antonio Escano, documented this miracle and led to obtaining a contract to construct a wooden tabernacle over the main altar.

At the base of the tabernacle, there is an opening for the "stone of the miracle." The opening was enclosed in a decorative case in a way that the people could see it.

To this day, the stone still has the imprint of the Hosts. [63]

---

[63] "Deepertruth: The Eucharistic Miracle of Mogoro Italy, 1604." Blog Talk Radio. <https://www.blogtalkradio.com/deeper-truth/2016/03/31/deepertruth-the-eucharistic-miracle-of-mogoro-italy-1604>. 12 July 2020.

The Miracle of Offida

The miracle of Offida took place in 1273 in the town of Lanciano when a woman named Richiarella was having trouble in her marriage.

She felt that her husband, Giacomo Stasio, was distancing himself from her so to win back his affection, she went to see a witch for advice. The witch told the woman to steal a consecrated Host to use in a love potion. The woman did as the witch had instructed her to do and stole the Host. When she got home, she put the Host on the fire in an earthenware jar.

However, when she threw the Host in the fire, the particles were transformed into living Flesh. The woman was terrified by the miracle so she wrapped the jar and the Miraculous Bloodies Host in a linen handkerchief and buried them under the manure in her husband's stable.

However, strange things began happening around their property. Every time that the husband's donkey entered the stable, it would genuflect towards the direction where the Host buried. The husband began to think that his wife had put a spell on the animal. Seven years passed and the wife felt remorse more and more as time passed.

Finally, she confessed her unspeakable sacrilege to the prior Augustinian priory in Lanciano, Giacomo Diotallevi.

The woman was crying and told the priest that she had killed God. The priest followed the woman to the stable and found the relics and the Host. The priest retrieved the Host and took the Blessed Sacrament back to his monastery.

Two monks hired a craftsman to create a cross-shaped reliquary. The monks asked the craftsman to not tell anybody what he was about to see and place inside the cross. The craftsman accepted and took the pyx containing the miraculous Host.

However, the craftsman was stricken with a sudden fever and asked the monks what they had brought them. The monks asked the craftsman if he was in mortal sin to which he responded that he was. The craftsman confessed his sins and his fever left immediately. It was then that he was able to hold the pyx without and danger. The craftsman didn't remove the Host but instead fixed the Host and the pyx together with the sacred wood inside the cross with a crystal above.

Today, the reliquaries of the jar and the Blood-stained linen with the cross containing the miraculous Host are exposed in the Church of St. Augustine in Offida. At the same time, Richiaretta's house was transformed into a small chapel.

Since then, the people of Offida and pilgrims celebrate the anniversary of the miracle there. [64]

---

[64] "Three extraordinary miracles of the Eucharist – Santarem, Amsterdam & Offida." Miracles of the Eucharist – Eucharistic Miracles of Santarem, Amsterdam, and Offida. Miracles of the Church. < https://www.miraclesofthechurch.com/2010/11/miracles-of-eucharist-eucharistic.html>. 12 July 12, 2020.

The Miracles of Rome

There are two main Eucharistic miracles that took place in Rome.

The first miracle occurred somewhere between the 6th century and the 7th century. One Sunday, St. Gregory was celebrating Mass at the church dedicated to St. Peter. While he was distributing Holy Communion, he saw a woman laughing.

During that time, parishioners were tasked to prepare the bread that was used as the Hosts during Mass.

Therefore, since she was one of the ones who made the bread, she didn't believe that it was actually Jesus' body. The pope was troubled and angered so he approached the woman and asked her to explain her behavior.

The woman told him that she herself had made the bread that the priest consecrated so there was no way that the bread was the actual Body of Christ.

Therefore, St. Gregory denied her Holy Communion and asked God to enlighten her and increase her faith.

Immediately, part of the bread that the woman had prepared became real Flesh and Blood. The woman repented and knelt on the ground crying.

Today, the relic of the miracle can be found in

Anechs, Germany, near the local Benedictine monastery.

The second Eucharistic Miracle in one of the oldest churches in Rome. The church has a small chapel known as the Caetani Chapel. This miracle involved a priest who was having doubts about Jesus' real presence in the Eucharist.

Therefore, he was not careful about taking great care of the Blessed Sacrament. So while saying Mass one day, he unintentionally let the Host fall on the ground while consecrating the Host. When the priest picked up the Host, he saw that the Host had left an imprint on the steps of the altar.

The imprint is still visible today. [65]

---

[65] "Eucharistic Miracle of Rome." The Eucharistic Miracles of the World. The Real Presence: Christ in the Eucharist. < http://therealpresence.org/eucharst/mir/english_pdf/Rome1.pdf>. 13 July 2020.

"Eucharistic Miracle of Rome." The Eucharistic Miracles of the World. The Real Presence: Christ in the Eucharist. <http://therealpresence.org/eucharst/mir/english_pdf/Rome3.pdf>. 13 July 2020.

The Miracle with St. Peter Damian

The miracle was witnessed and documented by a Father of the Church, St. Peter Damian, in 1050.

A young woman was instructed by a witch to steal a sacred Host to use in witchcraft. The young woman was naïve about the real presence of Jesus in the Eucharist. So the woman agreed and decided to steal a consecrated Host the following day. When the woman received Holy Communion, she hid the Host inside of her handkerchief and immediately headed for the exit.

However, the priest saw that she hid the Blessed Sacrament and followed to retrieve the Host.

The priest demanded her to give him back the Host. The woman was scared and nervous so she took out the handkerchief.

When the woman opened her handkerchief, she saw that the Host had been transformed.

Half of the Host remained in its natural form but the other half had become flesh that was bleeding.[66]

---

[66] "Eucharistic Miracle of St. Peter Damian ITALY – 11th Century." Our Lady of Lourdes & St. Swithun's Org. < https://stswithuns.org.uk/eucharistic-miracles-of-saint-damian>. 13 July 13, 2020.

The Miracles of Scala

The Eucharistic Miracle of Scala took place in a Monastery of the Most Holy Redeemer by Venerable Sister Maria Celeste Crostarosa and St. Alphonsus Maria Liguori.

One of their prayers involved having the Most Blessed Sacrament exposed in the monastery for public adoration.

The first miracle took place on September 11, 1732 and lasted for three consecutive months. During the exposition, signs of the Passion of Christ appeared in the Host contained in the monstrance.

Many people witnessed the Eucharistic Phenomenon including the villagers, nuns, Bishop Santoro of Scala, Bishop of Castellamare, St. Alphonsus Maria Liguori, and Bishop Santoro. [67]

---

[67] "Eucharistic Miracle of Scala." The Eucharistic Miracles of the World. The Real Presence: Christ in the Eucharist. < http://therealpresence.org/eucharst/mir/english_pdf/Damian-Scala.pdf>. 13 July 13, 2020.

The Miracles of Salzano

The Eucharistic Miracle of Salzano occurred in August 1536 when a priest, Fr. Lorenzo, was called to administer Holy Communion to a dying man.

It was late at night and the season was terrible so the priest wasn't able to take a procession with him so he only took an altar boy to help him. When they arrived at the meadows surrounding the Muson River, they found several donkeys eating at a pasture.

As soon as the donkeys saw the priest, they began to follow him.

When the donkeys reached the priest, they bowed their knees and followed the priest with the Blessed Sacrament all the way to the dying man's house. When they reached the man's house, the donkeys again bowed their heads and genuflected in front of the Blessed Sacrament.

When the priest and the altar boy returned, the donkeys followed them until they reached the pasture where they had been eating. [68]

---

[68] "Eucharistic Miracle of Salzano." The Eucharistic Miracles of the World. Miracoli Eucaristici.org. < http://www.miracolieucaristici.org/en/Liste/list.html>. 13 July 2020.

The Miracles of Trani

The Eucharistic Miracle of Trani took place around the 11th century. In this case, a satanic woman and her fellow satanic worshippers stole a consecrated Host with the intention of desecrating the Host and mock God. When the woman received Holy Communion, she took out the Host from her mouth and unto a handkerchief. When the woman got home, she threw the consecrated Host into a frying pan.

As soon as the Host touched the boiling oil, the Host became bloody flesh and hemorrhage that kept flowing that the blood burst into the woman's face and her house. The woman began to scream in fright causing her neighbors to run into her house. The archbishop was informed immediately and ordered that the Host be returned to the same church.

In 1616, the relic of the Host was transferred to an antique silver shrine. The house of the woman was turned into a chapel in 1706.

Today, the Host is housed in the Cathedral of Holy Mary of the Assumption. [69]

---

[69] "Eucharistic Miracle of Trani." The Eucharistic Miracles of the World. Miracoli Eucaristici.org. < http://www.miracolieucaristici.org/en/Liste/scheda.html?nat=italia&wh=trani&ct=Trani, XI sec.>. 13 July 13, 2020.

The Miracles of Veroli

The Eucharistic Miracle of Veroli took place on Easter in 1570 in the Church of St. Erasmus. During this time, the consecrated Host placed in a round silver pyx and placed in a burse-like holder. Later on, this was placed in a large, ceremonial silver chalice with its paten wrapped in an elegant silk cloth.

One night during the exposition of the Blessed Sacrament, people saw a strong dazzling light at the base of the chalice's cup, and above the star – which was attached to the Blessed Sacrament. The vision ended when small luminous child-like angels appeared in adoration around the Host.

The chalice, its paten, and the silver pyx, where the Blessed Sacrament was exposed, have been preserved and they remain with the relics. Unfortunately, the miraculous Host was consumed after 112 years. This miraculous miracle is commemorated with a solemn ceremony in the presence of the bishop [70]

---

[70] "Eucharistic Miracle of Veroli." The Eucharistic Miracles of the World. Miracoli Eucaristici.org. < http://www.miracolieucaristici.org/en/Liste/scheda.html?nat=italia&wh=veroli&ct=Veroli, 1570>. 13 July 2020.

The Miracles of Volterra

The Eucharistic Miracle of Volterra took place in 1472 during an Allumiere war.

During the war, soldiers looted and sacked the city of Volterra. One soldier broke into a church and went directly to the tabernacle. The soldier stole the ciborium, which still contained sacred Hosts, along with other sacred objects. As soon as he left the church, he felt a strong hatred against Jesus in the Holy Eucharist.

So in his hatred, he threw the ciborium against an external wall of the church. The Hosts immediately came out as if they were being held by an invisible force. The Hosts were then elevated into the air and radiating with light. The man was frightened and fell to his knees. The soldier repented and began to cry.

This event was witnessed by the townspeople and Friar Biagio Lisci.[71]

---

[71] "Eucharistic Miracle of Volterra." The Eucharistic Miracles of the World. Miracoli Eucaristici.org. < http://www.miracolieucaristici.org/en/Liste/scheda.html?nat=italia&wh=veroli&ct=Veroli, 1570>. 13 July 2020.

The Miracle of Alkmaar

The miracle of Alkmaar took place in the Cathedral of Saint Lawrence on May 1, 1429. On that day, a newly ordained priest, Fr. Folkert, was celebrating his first Mass. After he had consecrated the bread and wine into the Body and Blood of Jesus Christ, he accidentally knocked over the chalice. The wine turned into the real living blood of Christ. The priest panicked but didn't know what to do so he continued saying Mass. After Mass, the priest panicked so he cut off part of the chasuble that was stained with the Blood and burnt it. He took the rest of the chasuble and began to sow the ripped part.

However, as soon as he finished sowing it, the Bloodstain appeared again. The priest and the pastor, Fr. Volpert Schult, didn't know what to do so they immediately took the chasuble to the Bishop of Utrech.

There were many investigations done on the chasuble and in 1433, the bishop officially approved the devotion to this miracle.[72]

---

[72] "Eucharistic Miracle of Alkmaar." The Eucharistic Miracles of the World. The Real Presence: Christ in the Eucharist. < http://therealpresence.org/eucharst/mir/english_pdf/Alkmaar.pdf>. 13 July 2020.

"Eucharistic Miracles (1400-1500)." The Miracle Hunter.
<http://www.miraclehunter.com/eucharistic-miracles/1400-1500.html>. 13 July 13, 2020.

The Miracle of Boxmeer

The miracle of Boxmeer took place in 1400 in the church of Saints Peter and Paul when Fr. Arnoldus Groen was celebrating Mass. After he had consecrated the bread and wine into the Body and Blood of Christ, he began to doubt that Jesus was present in the Holy Eucharist. The Precious Blood immediately began to boil and began to bubble out of the chalice and onto the corporal. The priest repented and asked God to forgive him. The Precious Blood then stopped bubbling and transformed into dry coagulated blood as big as a walnut.

Today, the miraculous relics of the corporal and the Precious Blood are preserved and displayed. On the anniversary of the miracle, the people celebrate it with an annual solemn procession.[73]

---

[73] "Eucharistic Miracles (1400-1500)." The Miracle Hunter. <http://www.miraclehunter.com/eucharistic-miracles/1400-1500.html>. 13 July 2020.

The Miracle of Bergen

The miracle of Bergen happened 1421 during the Sunday before the Feast of Pentecost. The pastor of the Church of Saints Peter and Paul did not believe that Jesus was present in the Holy Eucharist. So after Mass, he threw the consecrated Hosts that were leftover from Mass into a canal.

After several months passed, fishermen found the Hosts floating in the water. When the fishermen picked up the Hosts, they saw that the Hosts contained coagulated Blood.

News of the miraculous recovery of the Hosts spread quickly and pilgrims began visiting the miraculous Hosts. The bishop approved the devotion but banned it while the Protestant Reformation took place. However, Catholics still honored the devotion in secret. Finally, in the 20th century, the devotion was restored and pilgrims still make pilgrimages to honor the miraculous Hosts.[74]

---

[74] "Eucharistic Miracle of Bergen." The Eucharistic Miracles of the World. The Real Presence: Christ in the Eucharist. < http://therealpresence.org/eucharst/mir/english_pdf/Bergen.pdf>. 13 July 2020.

"Eucharistic Miracles (1400-1500)." The Miracle Hunter.
<http://www.miraclehunter.com/eucharistic-miracles/1400-1500.html>. 13 July 13, 2020.

The Miracles of Meerssen

Meerssen is known for two important Eucharistic Miracles that took place in the same church.

The first miracle happened in 1222 when a priest consecrated the Eucharist. When the time came to break the Host, living Blood began to drip from the large Host and into corporal. The corporal was then placed in public view for people to venerate the Precious Living Blood that stained the corporal.

The other miracle took place in 1465 when a fire broke out and destroyed the church.

However, a farmer was able to break in and rescue the Blood-stained Host before it was ever damaged. The townspeople called this "Miracle of the Fire." The church was immediately rebuilt and in 1938, Pope Pius XI promoted the church to a minor basilica.

To this day, this basilica remains a center of pilgrimage where the precious relic of the miracle is carried in procession each year on the octave of Corpus Christi.[75]

---

[75] "Eucharistic Miracle of Meerssen." Foundation: Mary Pages.
<https://www.marypages.com/eucharistic-miracle-of-meerssen-en.html>. 13 July 13, 2020.

The Miracle of Stiphout

The miracle of Stiphout happened in 1342 when a vicious thunderstorm hit the village of Stiphout. A lightning bolt struck the parish and set it on fire. The fire spread quickly throughout the church.

The pastor, Jan Hocaerts, ran to warn his neighbors about the fire. A church member, Jan Baloys, heard about the fire and immediately went to the church to rescue the Most Blessed Sacrament.

The entrance was blocked so he lowered himself through a window to get inside. When he entered the church, he saw that the fire had engulfed the whole church – except for the tabernacle. The fire was prevented from reaching the tabernacle so Jan quickly opened the tabernacle, grabbed the ciborium, and exited the burnt church. The event was called a miracle and the church was quickly rebuilt.

Unfortunately, after 1557, there were many religious revolts, wars, etc. so all the Hosts were lost.[76]

---

[76] "The Guardian Angel: Eucharistic Miracle of Stiphout, 1342." Deeper Truth Blog: Catholic Perspectives on Everyday Life. 30 March 2020. < https://www.deepertruthcatholics.com/single-post/2020/03/30/The-Guardian-Angel-Eucharistic-Miracle-of-Stiphout-1342>. 13 July 2020.

The Miracle of Glotowo

The miracle of Glotowo took place in the 13th century when the Lithuanian troops invaded Poland. The parish priest was worried that the Blessed Sacrament would be defiled by the troops so he buried a consecrated Host in a gold-plated ciborium in a field outside of town. Nobody knew about the buried ciborium with the Host inside since the priest wasn't able to tell anybody.

However, in 1290, a farmer was plowing his field one day when he saw his oxen bowing to the ground in adoration. The farmer saw a blinding light shining from the ground in the middle of the oxen. The farmer began to dig and found the ciborium. He picked it up to inspect it and found the Host intact. The farmer was in awe and immediately took the Host to the church in Dobre Miastro.

News spread of the miracle and people went to the church to see the Miraculous Host for themselves. However, the Host disappeared and reappeared in the field again. The townspeople took it as a message to build a church there and dedicate it to Corpus Christi.[77]

---

[77] "Glotowo, Poland: Eucharistic Miracle of Glotowo" The Catholic Travel Guide. <https://thecatholictravelguide.com/destinations/poland/glotowo-poland-eucharistic-miracle-glotowo/>. 13 July 2020.

The Miracle of Krakow

The miracle of Krakow took place on August 14, 1730, near Krakow. The miracle began when some thieves broke into a church, The Collegiate Church of All Saints), and stole the monstrance that contained consecrated Hosts. The thieves got away but later on, they threw away the monstrance in a muddy marshland when they discovered that it was not real gold.

The priests and the townspeople began to search for the consecrated Hosts for a long time but were not able to find them. However, when it got dark, the place where the ciborium was dumped began to emanate a bright light. The Host produced flashes of light that were visible for several miles. The townspeople approached the area but they were too afraid to pick up the ciborium so they reported the event to the Bishop of Krakow.

The bishop called for three days of fasting and prayer. Finally, on the third day, the bishop led a procession out to where the ciborium had been ditched. When they arrived, they found the monstrance and the Hosts inside. The Hosts were intact and found to be the source of the illuminating lights. The people continue to celebrate this miracle every year on the feast of Corpus Christi in the church of Corpus Christi in Krakow.[78]

---

[78] "The Eucharistic miracle in Krakow." Catholics Say. <https://catholicsay.com/the-eucharistic-miracle-in-krakow/>. 14 July 2020.

The Miracle of Poznan

The miracle of Poznan happened when profaners decided to desecrate the Blessed Sacrament. The profaners persuaded one of their servants to steal three consecrated Hosts and promised her a large reward if she did so. The woman agreed and was able to steal three consecrated Hosts.

As soon as the profaners received the Hosts, they went to the basement of their mansion and began to desecrate the Hosts. The men put the Hosts on a table and began to stab the Eucharist with knives and other pointed objects.

The Hosts immediately began to bleed and splashed everywhere. Some of the Blood fell on the face of a blind girl.

The girl was immediately cured and received back her sight. The men were scared and so they decided to destroy the Hosts.

However, no matter what they did, they could not destroy the Hosts. So the men decided to take the consecrated Hosts outside of the city and threw them into a marsh near the Warta River.

A shepherd was walking by the march when he saw the three Hosts illuminating a bright light and suspended in the air. The shepherd was frightened and didn't know what to do so he returned home and reported everything that he had seen to his family and the local authorities. However, the burgomaster didn't believe him nor did he care so he ordered the shepherd to be jailed. Nevertheless, the shepherd was able to escape but returned to the burgomaster to tell him again. When the shepherd was able to convince the burgomaster, the burgomaster decided to follow him to the marsh.

Meanwhile, the townspeople had already gathered around the three miraculous Hosts. However, nobody was able to retrieve them no matter what they did.

It was only when Bishop Wojciech Jastrzebiec, arrived and prayed to God to be able to retrieve them. God heard his prayer and the Hosts descended into the pyx that he was holding. The bishop directed a solemn procession to accompany the miraculous Hosts to St. Mary Magdalene Church.

Soon afterward, a wooden chapel was constructed in the marsh where many pilgrims from all over visited.

One of those pilgrims was King Wladyslaw Jagiello who ordered a church to be a built and dedicated it to the Body of Christ (Corpus Domini).

In the 19th century, a shrine was constructed in the mansion where the desecration of the Hosts had taken place. Since then, a procession is held every Thursday with the Holy Eucharist at the Corpus Domini Church. The table where the Hosts had been desecrated is on display where the imprints of the Blood that dripped from the Hosts. [79]

---

[79] "The Guardian Angel: Eucharistic Miracle Poznam, Poland 1399." Deeper Truth Blog: Catholic Perspectives on Everyday Life. <https://www.deepertruthcatholics.com/single-post/2017/07/19/The-Guardian-Angel-Eucharistic-Miracle-Poznam-Poland-1399>. 14 July 2020.

The Miracle of Assisi

The miracle of Assisi took place with the help of Saint Clare at the convent of San Damiano in Assisi, Italy. During this time, the Saracen soldiers had taken place of the city and were looting everything they could find. Soon, they focused their attention on the convent of San Damiano. The soldiers broke into the convent and into the cloister where the nuns lived.

The nuns were hiding in the chapel crying out to God for help. St. Clare was divinely inspired to face them with the Holy Eucharist. She took the silver and ivory case that contained the Blessed Sacrament. She prostrated herself in front of the Eucharist and prayed to God for protection.

All of a sudden, they heard the voice of Jesus coming from the tabernacle saying that He would always protect them. Jesus had comforted St. Clare and given her the strength to comfort her sisters in return.

When the soldiers broke into the chapel, St. Clare held a monstrance with the Blessed Sacrament inside it. As soon as the soldiers saw the Blessed Sacrament, they fled in terror from the convent and from the city. [80]

---

[80] Stephen, Ryan. "There are 22 Eucharistic Miracles in Italy. The Powerful Sign of God on our 'Distracted' Nation." Mystic Post. 23 May 2018. < https://mysticpost.com/2018/05/oolthere-are-22-eucharistic-miracles-in-italy-the-powerful-sign-of-god-on-our-distracted-nation/>. 14 July 2020.

The Miracle of Alboraya-Almácera

The miracle of Alboraya-Almácera took place in 1348 when a priest was taking Holy Communion to a village where there were many sick people. The priest was carrying a ciborium that contained many Hosts. As he was crossing the river on the back of a mule, the water from the river came rushing in. The priest slipped from the mule and dropped the ciborium containing the Hosts causing them to be carried away by the river. The priest was barely able to save himself but he felt remorse for not being able to protect the Hosts.

Some fishermen came to his aid and told the priest that where the river flowed into the sea, there were fish holding the Hosts with their mouth. The priest immediately ran back to the church and returned to the river holding a new ciborium. The priest was amazed and filled with joy when he returned to the river and saw that the fish were still in the river with their heads sticking out of the water and still holding the Hosts. The priest fell down to his knees and extended the chalice out towards the river. The priest prayed to God fervently and the fish approached him with the Eucharist. The fish carefully placed the Hosts in the ciborium and then jumped back into the river. As soon as the priest stood up, he realized that a group of people was standing around him observing the whole event. [81]

---

[81] "Guardian Angel: Eucharistic Miracle of Alboraya-Almacera Spain 1348." Deeper Truth Blog: Catholic Perspectives on Everyday Life. 21 October 2019.
<https://www.deepertruthcatholics.com/single-post/2019/10/21/Guardian-Angel-Eucharistic-Miracle-of-Alboraya-Almacera-Spain-1348>. 14 July 2020.

Jesus in the Eucharistic

The Miracle of Alcoy

The miracle of Alcoy took place on January 29, 1568, when a man, Juan Prats, broke into a church and stole many sacred objects – including a precious silver box that contained three consecrated Hosts.

The man found the three Hosts when he opened the box and consumed them immediately and then hid the box in his stable. The man was filled with remorse so he went to the parish priest, Don Antonio, and told him about his sin.

The priest immediately sounded the church bells to let the people know about the dreadful sin. The people gathered in the church and began to pray earnestly. A search for the stolen Hosts was held but nobody was able to find them.

Meanwhile, there was a pious woman named María Miralles who was praying profoundly in front of a statue of Baby Jesus asking for the return of the Hosts. The statue of the Baby Jesus began to move and his finger pointed to the house of her neighbor, Juan Prats. The woman was too scared to confront the man so she went to the civil authorities and to tell them what she saw.

The priest was among those present and when he heard her story, a mysterious force led him to Juan Prats' home.

When the priest reached Juan Prats' property, he was led to the stable and began to rummage through the pile of wood. The priest immediately found the silver box and when he opened it, he saw three consecrated Hosts.

Juan Prats was confused because he knew that he had consumed the Hosts.

The miracle is still celebrated by the people of Alcoy in a festival that is celebrated on the feast of Corpus Christi.

Today, the statue of the Baby Jesus is kept in the Monastery of the Holy Sepulcher of Alcoy and the house of Juan Prats was turned into an oratory.[82]

---

[82] "Eucharistic Miracles (1500-1600)." The Miracle Hunter.
<http://www.miraclehunter.com/eucharistic-miracles/1500-1600.html>. 14 July 2020.

The Miracle of Caravaca de la Cruz

The miracle of Caravaca de la Cruz took place in May 1232. A priest, Don Gínes Pérez Chirinos de Cuenca traveled to the Moors of the Kingdom of Murcia to preach the Gospel. Unfortunately, the Moorish King Zeyt-Abu-Zeyt had him arrested.

However, the king was curious about the Christian faith and the importance of Mass. The priest explained the importance of Mass and the miraculous Blessed Sacrament. Curious, the king ordered the priest to celebrate Mass immediately.

However, the priest didn't have the necessary equipment to celebrate Mass so the King ordered his servants to go to the country of Cuenca, which was a Christian Territory. The servants returned with all the necessary equipment but forgot to bring a crucifix.

The priest was disturbed that the crucifix wasn't there so the king asked him what was bothering him. The priest told him that the crucifix was missing.

However, the king pointed towards the altar and showed him that two angels had appeared and were placing a crucifix one upon the altar.

The priest was grateful to God and gladly celebrated Mass. When the time for consecration came, the priest held the Host in the air.

While the priest was holding the Host, the king and those present saw Baby Jesus looking at him with a gaze of endearment.

The king and his family immediately converted to Christianity and were baptized. The king took the name of Vincent and his wife took the name of Elena.

The Catholic Church recognizes the fragment Caravaca as the Vera Cruz, a title for the cross that was found by Saint Isabel, the mother of Constantine. [83]

---

[83] "Eucharistic Miracle of Caravaca de la Cruz 1231 (Spain)." Our Lady of Lourdes & St Swithun's.
< https://stswithuns.org.uk/tag/eucharistic-miracle-of-caravaca-de-la-cruz-1231/>. 14 July 14, 2020.

The Miracle of Cimballa

The miracle of Cimbala took place in 1370 in the Church of the Purification of Our Lady.

The pastor, Don Tommaso, unfortunately, had serious doubts about the true presence of Jesus in the Most Blessed Sacrament. While he was saying Mass, the priest raised the Host in the air as he recited the prayers of consecration. As he was still holding the Host, the Host turned into real Flesh and Blood began to flow from the Host and unto the altar. The priest fell to his knees and began to cry from remorse. Those present saw the priest's reaction so they approached the altar and witnessed the miracle for themselves.

Since then, the Host produced many miracles and got the name: "Most Holy Doubtful Mystery."

Since then, the relic of the bloodstained altar linen has been exposed on the anniversary of the miracle on the 12th of September every year. [84]

---

[84] "Eucharistic Miracle of Cimbala." The Eucharistic Miracles of the World. The Real Presence: Christ in the Eucharist. < http://therealpresence.org/eucharst/mir/english_pdf/Cimballa.pdf>. 14 July 2020.

The Miracle of Daroca

In 1239, the Spanish and the Moors were at war with each other. So far, the Moors were winning and taking a lot of territory from the Spanish. The Christian cities of Daroca, Teruel, and Calatayud had allied together and were about to conquer the castle of Chio Luchente.

Before the first battle, the chaplain, Don Mateo Martínez of Daroca, celebrated Mass with the six captains: Don Jiménez Pérez, Don Fernando Sánchez, Don Pedro, Don Raimundo, Don Guillermo, and Don Simone Carroz. The priest took six Hosts meant for the six captains. As soon as the priest said the prayers of consecration, the Moors launched a surprise attack on them. The priest didn't want the enemy to desecrate the Hosts so he coiled the six Hosts in a corporal and hid them under a rock.

The Spanish were able to defeat the enemy and afterward, they asked the priest to give them Holy Communion to thank God for their victory.

Don Mateo took the men to the place where he had hidden the corporal to retrieve the Hosts. However, when the priest took the Hosts out of the corporal, he found that the Hosts were drenched in Blood. The Spanish took that as a sign that God was on their side.

The generals received Holy Communion and tied the Blood-stained corporal to a spear to make a banner.

The Spanish took the miraculous banner into battle with them and were miraculously able to reconquer Castle of Chio. Their triumphant win was attributed to the Eucharistic miracle. The six commanders went to different regions of Spain and began to command that the corporal be kept in their cities.

The church began to discuss the matter and the city of Daroca was chosen to be the place of the miracle. However, they couldn't decide what city should be in possession of the corporal. Therefore, they decided to place the corporal on the back of a bull and let the bull wander freely. They decided that the city where the mule stopped would be chosen by God's Divine Will and the place where the corporal should reside. The mule traveled for twelve days for about 200 miles.

Finally, the bull stopped at the Church of Saint Mark in Daroca. They realized that that was the place where God had chosen.

Soon, they constructed a church and dedicated to Our Lady along with the miraculous corporal where it resides to this day. [85]

---

[85] Lane, Tommy. "Eucharistic Miracle of Daroca." Father Tommy Lane. < https://frtommylane.com/homilies/pilgrimage/daroca_eucharistic_miracle.htm>. 14 July 2020.

The Miracle of Gerona

The miracle of Gerona took place in the church of the Benedictines of San Daniele in 1297.

While the priest was saying Mass, he began to have doubts about whether Jesus was really in the Eucharist or not. However, when the priest placed the Host on his mouth, he wasn't able to swallow the Blessed Sacrament. The priest took out the Blessed Sacrament from his mouth and saw that the Host had transformed into real flesh. The priest didn't know what to do with the miraculous Host, so he wrapped up the Host in the corporal and placed it on the corner of the altar. One of the nuns was watching the priest during Mass and saw that the priest had hidden something in the altar.

When Mass ended, the nun immediately went to the altar to see what the priest had hidden. The nun found the white cloth with great astonishment discovered that turned into real Flesh that was dripping with Blood. The nun asked the priest about the Eucharistic Miracle, So the priest told her that he had doubted that Jesus was really present in the Eucharist. The priest also told the nun that he wasn't able to swallow the Host because the Host had increased in size so much so that he couldn't swallow the Blessed Sacrament.

The priest retrieved the miraculous Host and placed the Blessed Sacrament in a reliquary.

Regrettably, the reliquary that contained the miraculous Host and the Blood-soaked corporal were destroyed during the civil war of 1936.

---

[86] "Eucharistic Miracle of Gerona." The Eucharistic Miracles of the World. The Real Presence: Christ in the Eucharist. < http://therealpresence.org/eucharst/mir/english_pdf/Gerona.pdf>. 14 July 14, 2020.

The Miracle of Gorkum - El Escorial

The miracle of Gorkum - El Escorial happened in Holland in 1572 when the followers of Ulrich Zwingli called the "Sea Beggars." After invading Gorkum, the conquerors began to loot the city and the cathedral. Some of them entered the cathedral and began striking the tabernacle with bolts of iron. When they broke it, they seized the monstrance that contained the Blessed Sacrament. The soldiers were protestant and hated the Catholic religion. Therefore, they threw the Host on the ground and trampled the Host with spiked boots that broke the Host into three different pieces. Blood began to flow from the Host and formed themselves into three small wounds shaped in the form of a loop.

One of them felt remorse and hatred towards this action warned the Canon Jean van der Delft. The Canon was able to take the Hosts to safety and gave the Hosts to King Philip II of Spain. The King placed the Blessed Sacrament under the care of the Monastery of San Lorenzo in El Escorial.

Today the miraculous Host, also known as "Sagrada Forma" (Sacred Form), is kept intact in the Royal Monastery of San Lorenzo in El. Escorial. Every September 29th to October 28th, there is are solemn festivities and processions in honor of the miracle. [87]

---

[87] "Eucharistic Miracle of Gorkum - El Escorial." The Eucharistic Miracles of the World. The Real Presence: Christ in the Eucharist.
<http://therealpresence.org/eucharst/mir/english_pdf/Escorial.pdf>. 15 July 2020.

The Miracle of Guadalupe

The miracle of Guadalupe took place in Guadalupe near the region of Toledo, Spain in 1420. The Venerable Don Pedro Cabañuelas was a very devout priest who had a strong devotion to the Holy Eucharist and spent many hours in adoration. Nevertheless, he was tempted into doubting the presence of Jesus in the Blessed Sacrament.

One day when he was celebrating Mass, he witnessed a Eucharistic Miracle that made his doubts disappear. During the consecration, he saw a dense cloud come down from above and settled itself above the altar until he was engulfed in the smoke and couldn't see anything. The priest prayed to God to remove whatever doubts he may have had concerning the Eucharist.

The smoke began to disappear slowly until it was completely gone. When the smoke left, the priest saw the Host that he was lifting was bleeding and the drops of Blood fell onto the chalice. Once the chalice was full of Blood, the Blood began to drip onto the corporal and on the pall. Before the priest could react, he heard a voice telling him to finish saying Mass and to not reveal what he had seen just yet. Once he was allowed to reveal the miracle, news of it began to spread everywhere.

The King of Castile, Don Juan II, and the Queen, Lady Maria of Aragon, heard about the miracle and became very devoted to the Holy Eucharist.

They also venerated the Venerable Father Pedro Cabañuelas so much that they asked to be buried close to him.

Today, the precious relics of the corporal and of the bloodied pall are on display on the church of Guadalupe. [88]

---

[88] "Eucharistic Miracle of Guadalupe." The Eucharistic Miracles of the World. Miracles List: The Eucharistic Miracles of the World.
<http://www.miracolieucaristici.org/en/Liste/scheda.html?nat=spagna&wh=guadalupe&ct=Guadalupe, 1420>. 15 July 2020.

The Miracle of Ivorra

The miracle of Ivorra took place at 1055 in Ivorra, Spain. During the eleventh century, there were Protestant movements that denied the real presence of Jesus in the Eucharist. This affected a priest, Bernat Oliver, from Ivorra to doubt the real presence of Jesus.

One day when he was celebrating Mass, he saw that the wine in the chalice had turned into real Blood and began to pour onto the altar cloth and flowed all the way down to the floor. The event was reported to the Bishop of Urgell, Saint Ermengol. When the bishop heard about the miracle, he began to investigate the miracle immediately.

Once he was able to verify the miracle, he reported the miracle directly to Pope Sergius IV in Rome. The event was fully accepted as an authentic miracle and the relics or the miracle along with the pontifical document were placed under the high altar of the Church of Ivorra and inaugurated in 1055 by the Bishop Guillem de Urgell.

Today, the sacred relics of the miracle are preserved in a gothic reliquary since 1426. [89]

---

[89] "The Guardian Angel: The Eucharistic Miracle of Ivorra Spain 1010." Deeper Truth Blog: Catholic Perspectives on Everyday Life. 11 November 2019.
<https://www.deepertruthcatholics.com/single-post/2019/11/11/The-Guardian-Angel-The-Eucharistic-Miracle-of-Ivorra-Spain-1010>. 15 July 2020.

The Miracle of Moncada

The miracle of Moncada took place in 1392 during the turbulent times when there was no accepted valid pope.

The confusion began when Pope Urban VI was elected on April 18, 1378. However, the French cardinals opposed the new pope.

The French cardinals wanted to have a French pope who would transfer the Holy See back to Avignon. There were many battles and disagreements about the office of the pope.

So, on September 20, 1378, they elected the antipope Clement VII. Those who followed the antipope tried to seize Rome but failed to do so. Therefore, they retreated to Avignon where Clement VII continued to act as the legitimate pontiff. Therefore, since there were two popes and they each ordained priests, people weren't sure who was a legitimate priest. This was also the case with many priests who didn't know whether their priesthood was legitimate or not. This affected them when it came to the Blessed Sacrament.

Some priests doubted that they had the ability to consecrate the Bread and Wine into Jesus' Body and Blood. One of these priests was Fr. Mosén Jaime Carrós. He wasn't sure whether he was a valid priest because the bishop who ordained him served the antipope.

Therefore, every time that he distributed Holy Community, he felt that he deceived the people by distributing unconsecrated Hosts. The priest prayed fervently to God to give him a sign to let him know that he was able to consecrate the bread and wine into His own Body and Blood.

God answered his prayer on Christmas Day, 1392 when he was celebrating Mass. On Christmas day, a woman named Angela Alpicat attended Mass with her five-year-old daughter, Inés. (Inés, would later on, be known as St. Inés de Moncada)

After Mass, Inés refused to leave the church. She begged her mother to let her stay a little longer so she could play with the child that the priest was holding during Mass.

The following day, Lady Angela went to church again and when the priest lifted the Host, Inés saw the child again in the priest's hands. When Mass ended, Lady Angela told the priest about her daughter's visions. The priest immediately asked Inés about the little boy. Inés answered his questions to his amazement but he wanted to test her a little bit more. So the priest invited Inés and her mother to church the following day.

The following day during Mass, the priest took two Hosts - but only one of them was consecrated. The priest showed the consecrated Host to the little girl and asked her what she saw.

The little girl exclaimed that she could see the face of Baby Jesus. Then the priest lifted the unconsecrated host and asked Inés the same question. Inés answered that all she could see was a white little disc. The priest was ecstatic and so was the community because this proved that the priest's ordination was valid. [90]

---

[90] "True Stories of Eucharistic Miracles." True Stories of Eucharistic Miracles. Life Site Ministries. < https://www.lifesiteministries.org/true-stories-of-eucharistic-miracles.html>. 15 July 15, 2020.

The Miracle of O'Cebreiro

The miracle of O'Cebreiro took place on a terribly cold day in 1300.

A Benedictine priest was celebrating Mass in a chapel beside the church of the convent of O'Cebreiro on a terribly snowy day. The weather was so bad with unceasing snow and freezing wind. Therefore, he thought that nobody had bothered going to church for Mass.

However, there was a farmer from Barxamaior, Juan Santín, who left the convent to attend Mass. Unfortunately, the priest did not believe in the real presence of Jesus in the Eucharist. Therefore, he loathed the farmer's sacrifice of goodwill. The priest was mad that he had to celebrate Mass but he was forced to continue.

Immediately after he said the words of consecration, the Host transformed into real Flesh and the wine changed into real Blood. There was so much Blood that the Blood began to overflow from the chalice and unto the corporal. The priest noticed that the head of a wooden statue of the Virgin Mary was leaning over towards him as if she was leaning in adoration.

The statue of the Virgin Mary became known as the "Madonna of the Sacred Miracle."

The miraculous Host was kept for almost two hundred years on the paten.

However, when Queen Isabella heard about the miracle, she immediately had a precious crystal shrine to hold the miraculous Host and the paten.

Today, the miraculous Host and paten are still exposed for people to admire and adore. However, every year of the feast of Corpus Christi (August 15 and September 8) the relics are taken in procession along with the Madonna. [91]

---

[91] "The Miracle of O Cebreiro and the Galician Holy Grail." Mundi Plus. 9 February 2017. < https://www.mundiplus.com/en/blog/el-milagro-de-o-cebreiro-y-del-santo-grial-gallego>. 15 July 15, 2020.

The Miracle of Silla

The miracle of Silla happened on March 25, 1907, feast of the Annunciation.

When Mass ended, Fr. Fernand Gomez, the pastor of the Church of Our Lady of the Angels, opened the tabernacle to get the Hosts for Holy Communion. However, he found that the silver ciborium with the consecrated Hosts was gone.

A search was arranged and the Hosts were found two days later in a garden hidden under a stone. When the priest learned about it, he held a solemn procession with the lost Hosts to the church.

In 1934, they realized that the Hosts had remained intact after all those years. The Archbishop of Valencia started a process to declare the preservation of the Hosts a miracle and sealed with wax the reliquary containing the Hosts. Regrettably, two years later the bishop's residence was burned down by the anarchists-communists, and the precious document was lost. [92]

---

[92] "Eucharistic Miracle of Silla." The Eucharistic Miracles of the World. Miracoli Eucaristici. < http://www.miracoli eucaristici .org/en/Liste/scheda.html?nat=spagna&wh=silla&ct=Silla, 1907>. 15 July 2020.

The Miracle of Zaragoza

The miracle of Zaragoza took place in 1427 when a woman was tricked by a Moorish evil sorcerer. The woman had visited the sorcerer asking for a "cure" her husband of his violent temper and treat her more gently.

The sorcerer told her that he could make her a spell but would need a consecrated Host. The woman did as she was told so she went to the Church of Saint Michael, went to confession and received the Eucharist.

When the woman received Holy Communion, she took the Holy Eucharist from her mouth, and hid the Host in a small coffer. Immediately after she left the church, she took the Host to the sorcerer.

When they opened the coffer, they saw a Baby surrounded by light instead of the Host. The sorcerer got frightened so he told the woman to take the coffer home, burn the Blessed Sacrament, and return with the ashes.

The woman obeyed and did as she was told and threw the coffer into the fire. The coffer burned but she saw that the Baby remained unharmed. The woman was now terrified so she ran out of her house to ask the sorcerer for help.

However, when the sorcerer heard the woman's story, he began to tremble in fear and believed that he would be punished for his evil deed.

They both decided to go to the cathedral to confess their sin to Bishop Don Alonso. The bishop consulted with other bishops and theologians of the diocese to discuss what actions they should take. Finally, they decided to take the Miraculous Baby in a solemn procession from the house of the woman to the cathedral.[93]

---

[93] "Eucharistic Miracle of Zaragoza." The Eucharistic Miracles of the World. Miracoli Eucaristici. <http://www.miracolieucaristici.org/en/Liste/scheda.html?nat=spagna&wh=zaragoza&ct=Zaragoza, 1427>. 15 July 2020.

The Bread of Life

There are many kinds of Eucharistic miracles where Jesus reminds us that He is truly the Living Bread and Wine that we receive at church.

Jesus loved us so much that He chose to remain with us even after His Death, Resurrection, and Ascension into Heaven. He remained with us to unite us to His body by transforming His Body and Blood as nourishment for us all.

However, it is hard for us to comprehend the mystery of the Eucharist and often times take the Sacrament for granted.

Many of us find it difficult to believe that the Communion wafers and wine that we receive during Mass could actually be the Body and Blood of Jesus Christ. Even priests find it difficult at times to believe that the bread and wine that they consecrate become Jesus Himself.

Therefore, Jesus has chosen certain people at certain times throughout history to remind us that He is present in the Bread and Wine. Jesus has performed these miracles during church as the priest says Mass or when there is great sacrilege done to the Eucharist.

Some of the miracles show how the Hosts are preserved from damage while other miracles turn the Host into real flesh that bleeds.

Not only do the Hosts turn to flesh and bleed for a few moments but they have remained intact ever since. The Hosts have remained in the same condition as when the miracle happened instead of decaying. This shows us how even after all these years, the Hosts continue to live since they are the Body and Blood of Jesus: the everlasting God.

The angels themselves wish that they could receive the Eucharist. However, as angels, they are not able to.

In the Eucharist, Jesus gathers us to be part of His Body to become one and join Him to Himself. Jesus became flesh and now He remains as bread with us. Through His suffering and death, Jesus took our sins unto Himself and sanctified His Body.

When we join in Mass, we share the same sacrifice of Jesus' Passion every single time we attend Mass and every single Mass ever said commemorates the same sacrifice.

Jesus' suffering and death were for us so that is why He left us the Sacrament of the Eucharist.

Therefore, angels are not able to receive Holy Communion since Jesus did not die to save them from damnation. However, the angels greatly honor and worship the Eucharist and that is why we call the Eucharist "The Bread of the Angels."

As stated before, we cannot see Jesus' glory in the bread and wine but the angels stand in adoration all day and all night – even when we forget and neglect that Jesus is physically waiting for us in every single church.

The angels continuously worship Jesus in the form of Bread and Wine. Being spiritual, they see Jesus in all His glory so they know that the bread and wine have become Jesus Himself.

As mere mortal and physical beings, we are not attuned to experience the spiritual realm as the angels are so it is hard to believe. This is why Jesus continues to remind us of His presence through Eucharistic Miracles. With these miracles, Jesus proves to us and reminds us that He is truly with us and will be with us until the end of time.

Printed in Dunstable, United Kingdom